I0439797

Adaptive Harvest Management

2010 Hunting Season

$15

American
Wigeon

MIGRATORY BIRD HUNTING
AND CONSERVATION STAMP

Void After
June 30, 2011

U.S. DEPARTMENT OF THE INTERIOR

Adaptive Harvest Management

2010 Hunting Season

PREFACE

The process of setting waterfowl hunting regulations is conducted annually in the United States (Blohm 1989). This process involves a number of meetings where the status of waterfowl is reviewed by the agencies responsible for setting hunting regulations. In addition, the U. S. Fish and Wildlife Service (USFWS) publishes proposed regulations in the Federal Register to allow public comment. This document is part of a series of reports intended to support development of harvest regulations for the 2010 hunting season. Specifically, this report is intended to provide waterfowl managers and the public with information about the use of adaptive harvest management (AHM) for setting waterfowl hunting regulations in the United States. This report provides the most current data, analyses, and decision-making protocols. However, adaptive management is a dynamic process and some information presented in this report will differ from that in previous reports.

Citation: U. S. Fish and Wildlife Service. 2010. Adaptive Harvest Management: 2010 Hunting Season. U. S. Department of Interior, Washington, D. C. 59 pp. Available online at http://www.fws.gov/migratorybirds/mgmt/AHM/AHM-intro.htm

ACKNOWLEDGMENTS

A working group comprised of representatives from the USFWS, the U. S. Geological Survey (USGS), the Canadian Wildlife Service (CWS), and the four Flyway Councils (Appendix A) was established in 1992 to review the scientific basis for managing waterfowl harvests. The working group, supported by technical experts from the waterfowl management and research communities, subsequently proposed a framework for adaptive harvest management, which was first implemented in 1995. The USFWS expresses its gratitude to the AHM Working Group and to the many other individuals, organizations, and agencies that have contributed to the development and implementation of AHM.

This report was prepared by the USFWS Division of Migratory Bird Management. G. S. Boomer and T. A. Sanders were the principal authors. Individuals that provided essential information or otherwise assisted with report preparation were G. Zimmerman (USFWS), N. Zimpfer (USFWS), M. Koneff (USFWS), K. Richkus (USFWS), J. Klimstra (USFWS), E. Silverman (USFWS), K. Magruder (USFWS) and P. Garrettson (USFWS). Comments regarding this document should be sent to the Chief, Division of Migratory Bird Management-USFWS, 4401 North Fairfax Drive, MS MSP-4107, Arlington, VA 22203.

We are grateful for the continuing technical support from F. A. Johnson, M. C. Runge, and J. A. Royle (USGS), and acknowledge that information provided by USGS in this report has not received the Director's approval and, as such, is provisional and subject to revision.

Cover art: 2010 Federal Duck stamp artist Robert Bealle's painting of an American Wigeon (*Anas americana*).

TABLE OF CONTENTS

LIST OF FIGURES

LIST OF TABLES

1 EXECUTIVE SUMMARY

In 1995 the U.S. Fish and Wildlife Service (USFWS) implemented the Adaptive Harvest Management (AHM) program for setting duck hunting regulations in the United States. The AHM approach provides a framework for making objective decisions in the face of incomplete knowledge concerning waterfowl population dynamics and regulatory impacts.

The AHM protocol is based on the population dynamics and status of three mallard (*Anas platyrhynchos*) stocks. Mid-continent mallards are defined as those breeding in the Waterfowl Breeding Population and Habitat Survey (WBPHS) strata 13–18, 20–50, and 75–77 plus mallards breeding in the states of Michigan, Minnesota, and Wisconsin (state surveys). The prescribed regulatory alternative for the Mississippi and Central Flyways depends exclusively on the status of these mallards. Eastern mallards are defined as those breeding in WBPHS strata 51–54 and 56 and breeding in the states of Virginia northward into New Hampshire (Atlantic Flyway Breeding Waterfowl Survey [AFBWS]). The regulatory choice for the Atlantic Flyway depends exclusively on the status of these mallards. Western mallards are defined as those birds breeding in WBPHS strata 1–12 (hereafter Alaska) and those birds breeding in the states of California and Oregon (state surveys). The regulatory choice for the Pacific Flyway depends exclusively on the status of these mallards.

Mallard population models are based on the best available information and account for uncertainty in population dynamics and the impact of harvest. Model-specific weights reflect the relative confidence in alternative hypotheses and are updated annually using comparisons of predicted and observed population sizes. For mid-continent mallards, current model weights favor the weakly density-dependent reproductive hypothesis (89%) and suggest some preference for the additive-mortality hypothesis (62%). For eastern mallards, virtually all of the weight is on models that have corrections for bias in estimates of survival or reproductive rates. Current model weights provide some support for the weakly density-dependent reproductive hypothesis (65%). By consensus, hunting mortality is assumed to be additive in eastern mallards. Unlike mid-continent and eastern mallards, we consider a single functional form to predict western mallard population dynamics but consider a wide range of parameter values each weighted relative to the support from the data.

For the 2010 hunting season, the USFWS is considering the same regulatory alternatives as last year. The nature of the restrictive, moderate, and liberal alternatives has remained essentially unchanged since 1997, except that extended framework dates have been offered in the moderate and liberal alternatives since 2002. Harvest rates associated with each of the regulatory alternatives have been updated based on band-reporting rate studies conducted since 1998. The expected harvest rates of adult males under liberal hunting seasons are 0.117 (SD = 0.020), 0.148 (SD = 0.042), and 0.115 (SD = 0.031) for mid-continent, eastern, and western mallards, respectively.

Optimal regulatory strategies for the 2010 hunting season were calculated using: (1) harvest-management objectives specific to each mallard stock; (2) the 2010 regulatory alternatives; and (3) current population models. Based on this year's survey results of 8.60 million mid-continent mallards, 3.73 million ponds in Prairie Canada, 0.763 million eastern mallards, and 1.05 million western mallards in Alaska (0.606 million) and California-Oregon (0.443 million), the optimal choice for all four flyways is the liberal regulatory alternative.

AHM concepts and tools are also being applied to help improve harvest management for several other waterfowl stocks. In the last year, significant progress has been made to adopt an adaptive management protocol to inform northern pintail (*Anas acuta*) harvest decisions for 2010. In addition, we continue to update our understanding of the harvest potential of scaup (*Aythya affinis, A. marila*) as this decision making framework continues to evolve with feedback from annual monitoring information.

2 BACKGROUND

The annual process of setting duck-hunting regulations in the United States is based on a system of resource monitoring, data analyses, and rule-making (Blohm 1989). Each year, monitoring activities such as aerial surveys and hunter questionnaires provide information on population size, habitat conditions, and harvest levels. Data collected from this monitoring program are analyzed each year, and proposals for duck-hunting regulations are developed by the Flyway Councils, States, and USFWS. After extensive public review, the USFWS announces regulatory guidelines within which States can set their hunting seasons.

In 1995, the USFWS adopted the concept of adaptive resource management (Walters 1986) for regulating duck harvests in the United States. This approach explicitly recognizes that the consequences of hunting regulations cannot be predicted with certainty and provides a framework for making objective decisions in the face of that uncertainty (Williams and Johnson 1995). Inherent in the adaptive approach is an awareness that management performance can be maximized only if regulatory effects can be predicted reliably. Thus, adaptive management relies on an iterative cycle of monitoring, assessment, and decision-making to clarify the relationships among hunting regulations, harvests, and waterfowl abundance.

In regulating waterfowl harvests, managers face four fundamental sources of uncertainty (Nichols et al. 1995a, Johnson et al. 1996, Williams et al. 1996):

(1) environmental variation – the temporal and spatial variation in weather conditions and other key features of waterfowl habitat; an example is the annual change in the number of ponds in the Prairie Pothole Region, where water conditions influence duck reproductive success;

(2) partial controllability – the ability of managers to control harvest only within limits; the harvest resulting from a particular set of hunting regulations cannot be predicted with certainty because of variation in weather conditions, timing of migration, hunter effort, and other factors;

(3) partial observability – the ability to estimate key population attributes (e.g., population size, reproductive rate, harvest) only within the precision afforded by extant monitoring programs; and

(4) structural uncertainty – an incomplete understanding of biological processes; a familiar example is the long-standing debate about whether harvest is additive to other sources of mortality or whether populations compensate for hunting losses through reduced natural mortality. Structural uncertainty increases contentiousness in the decision-making process and decreases the extent to which managers can meet long-term conservation goals.

AHM was developed as a systematic process for dealing objectively with these uncertainties. The key components of AHM include (Johnson et al. 1993, Williams and Johnson 1995):

(1) a limited number of regulatory alternatives, which describe Flyway-specific season lengths, bag limits, and framework dates;

(2) a set of population models describing various hypotheses about the effects of harvest and environmental factors on waterfowl abundance;

(3) a measure of reliability (probability or "weight") for each population model; and

(4) a mathematical description of the objective(s) of harvest management (i.e., an "objective function"), by which alternative regulatory strategies can be compared.

These components are used in a stochastic optimization procedure to derive a regulatory strategy. A regulatory strategy specifies the optimal regulatory choice, with respect to the stated management objectives, for each possible combination of breeding population size, environmental conditions, and model weights (Johnson et al. 1997). The setting of annual hunting regulations then involves an iterative process:

(1) each year, an optimal regulatory choice is identified based on resource and environmental conditions, and on current model weights;

(2) after the regulatory decision is made, model-specific predictions for subsequent breeding population size are determined;

(3) when monitoring data become available, model weights are increased to the extent that observations of population size agree with predictions, and decreased to the extent that they disagree; and

(4) the new model weights are used to start another iteration of the process.

By iteratively updating model weights and optimizing regulatory choices, the process should eventually identify which model is the best overall predictor of changes in population abundance. The process is optimal in the sense that it provides the regulatory choice each year necessary to maximize management performance. It is adaptive in the sense that the harvest strategy evolves to account for new knowledge generated by a comparison of predicted and observed population sizes.

3 MALLARD STOCKS AND FLYWAY MANAGEMENT

Since its inception AHM has focused on the population dynamics and harvest potential of mallards, especially those breeding in mid-continent North America. Mallards constitute a large portion of the total U.S. duck harvest, and traditionally have been a reliable indicator of the status of many other species. As management capabilities have grown, there has been increasing interest in the ecology and management of breeding mallards that occur outside the mid-continent region. Geographic differences in the reproduction, mortality, and migrations of mallard stocks suggest that there may be corresponding differences in optimal levels of sport harvest. The ability to regulate harvests of mallards originating from various breeding areas is complicated, however, by the fact that a large degree of mixing occurs during the hunting season. The challenge for managers, then, is to vary hunting regulations among Flyways in a manner that recognizes each Flyway's unique breeding-ground derivation of mallards. Of course, no Flyway receives mallards exclusively from one breeding area; therefore, Flyway-specific harvest strategies ideally should account for multiple breeding stocks that are exposed to a common harvest.

The optimization procedures used in AHM can account for breeding populations of mallards beyond the mid-continent region, and for the manner in which these ducks distribute themselves among the Flyways during the hunting season. An optimal approach would allow for Flyway-specific regulatory strategies, which represent an average of the optimal harvest strategies for each contributing breeding stock weighted by the relative size of each stock in the fall flight. This joint optimization of multiple mallard stocks requires: (1) models of population dynamics for all recognized stocks of mallards; (2) an objective function that accounts for harvest-management goals for all mallard stocks in the aggregate; and (3) decision rules allowing Flyway-specific regulatory choices.

Currently, three stocks of mallards are officially recognized for the purposes of AHM (Figure 1). We use a constrained approach to the optimization of these stocks' harvest, in which the Atlantic Flyway regulatory strategy is based exclusively on the status of eastern mallards, the regulatory strategy for the Mississippi and Central Flyways is based exclusively on the status of mid-continent mallards, and the Pacific Flyway regulatory strategy is based exclusively on the status of western mallards. This approach has been determined to perform nearly as well as a joint-optimization because mixing of the three stocks during the hunting season is limited and because of the constraints imposed by management objectives and regulatory alternatives.

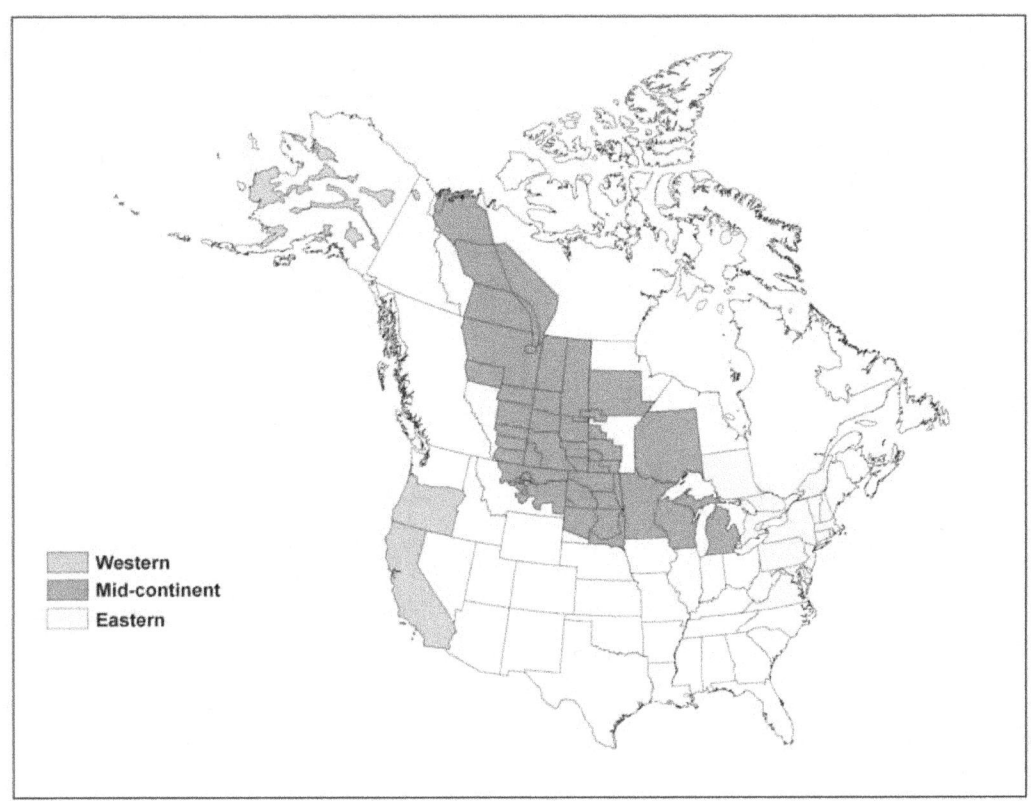

Figure 1 – Survey areas currently assigned to the mid-continent, eastern, and western stocks of mallards for the purposes of AHM.

4 MALLARD POPULATION DYNAMICS

4.1 Mid-Continent Stock

Mid-continent mallards are defined as those breeding in WBPHS strata 13–18, 20–50, and 75–77, and in the Great Lakes region (Michigan, Minnesota, and Wisconsin; see Figure 1). Estimates of the size of this population are available since 1992, and have varied from 6.4 to 11.2 million (Table B.1, Figure 2). Estimated breeding-population size in 2010 was 8.60 million (SE = 0.29 million), including 7.82 million (SE = 0.28 million) from the WBPHS and 0.780 million (SE = 0.059 million) from the Great Lakes region.

Details describing the set of population models for mid-continent mallards are provided in Appendix B. The set consists of four alternatives, formed by the combination of two survival hypotheses (additive vs. compensatory hunting mortality) and two reproductive hypotheses (strongly vs. weakly density dependent). Relative weights for the alternative models of mid-continent mallards changed little until all models under-predicted the change in population size from 1998 to 1999, perhaps indicating there is a significant factor affecting population dynamics that is absent from all four models (Figure 3). Updated model weights suggest some preference for the additive-mortality models (62%) over those describing hunting mortality as compensatory (38%). For most of the time frame, model weights have strongly favored the weakly density-dependent reproductive models over the strongly density-dependent ones, with current model weights of 89% and 11%, respectively. The reader is cautioned, however, that models can sometimes make reliable predictions of population size for reasons having little to do with the biological hypotheses expressed therein (Johnson et al. 2002b).

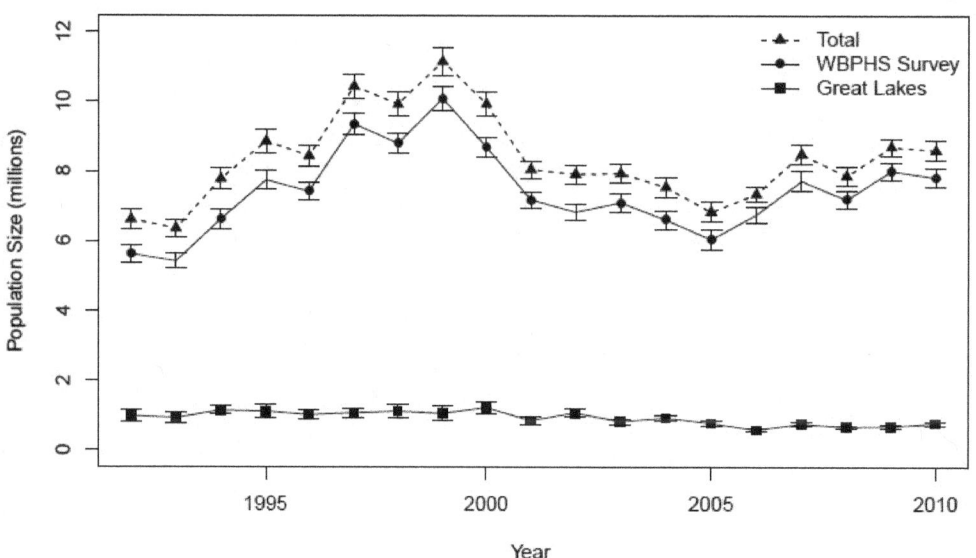

Figure 2 – Population estimates of mid-continent mallards observed in the WBPHS (strata: 13–18, 20–50, and 75–77) and the Great Lakes region (Michigan, Minnesota, and Wisconsin). Error bars represent one standard error.

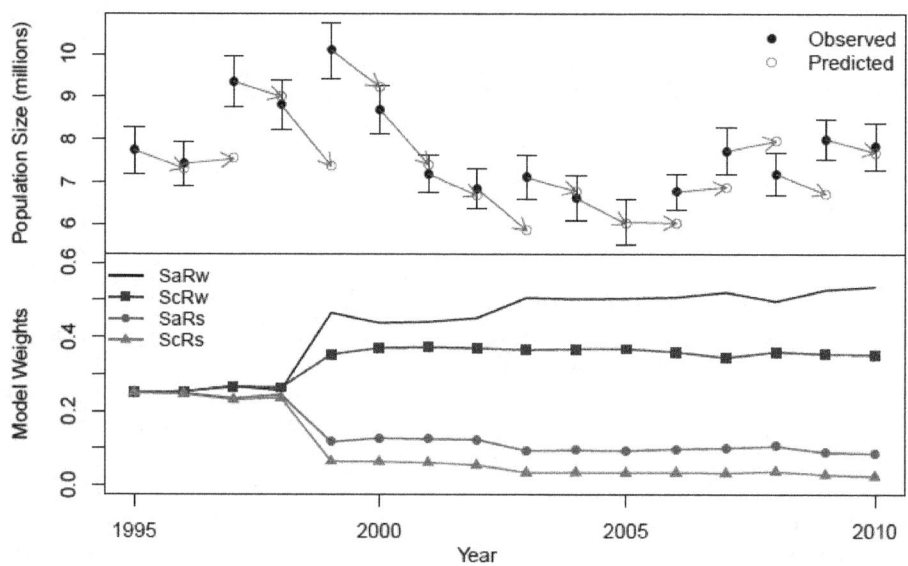

Figure 3 – Top panel: population estimates of mid-continent mallards observed in the WBPHS compared to mid-continent mallard model set predictions (weighted average based on 2010 model weights) from 1996 to 2010. Error bars represent 95% confidence intervals. Bottom panel: mid-continent mallard model weights (SaRw = additive mortality and weakly density-dependent reproduction, ScRw = compensatory mortality and weakly density-dependent reproduction, SaRs = additive mortality and strongly density-dependent reproduction, ScRs = compensatory mortality and strongly density-dependent reproduction). Model weights were assumed to be equal in 1995.

4.2 Eastern Stock

Eastern mallards are defined as those breeding in southern Ontario and Quebec (WBPHS strata 51–54 and 56) and in the northeastern U.S. (AFBWS; Heusmann and Sauer 2000, see Figure 1). Estimates of population size have varied from 0.76 to 1.1 million since 1990, with the majority of the population accounted for in the northeastern U.S. (Table C.1, Figure 4). For 2010, the estimated breeding-population size of eastern mallards was 0.763 million (SE = 0.053 million), including 0.653 million (SE = 0.049 million) from the northeastern U.S. and 0.110 million (SE = 0.021 million) from the WBPHS. The reader is cautioned that these estimates differ from those reported in the USFWS annual waterfowl trend and status reports, which include composite estimates based on more fixed-wing strata in eastern Canada and helicopter surveys conducted by the Canadian Wildlife Service (CWS).

Details concerning the set of population models for eastern mallards are provided in Appendix C. The set consists of six alternatives, formed by the combination of two reproductive hypotheses (strongly vs. weakly density dependent) and three hypotheses concerning bias in estimates of survival and reproductive rates (no bias vs. biased survival rates vs. biased reproductive rates). With respect to model weights, there is no single model that is clearly favored over the others at the current time. Collectively, current model weights provide some support for the weakly density-dependent reproductive hypotheses 65% compared to the strongly density dependent reproductive hypotheses 35% (Figure 5). In addition, there is overwhelming evidence of bias in extant estimates of survival or reproductive rates, assuming that survey estimates are unbiased.

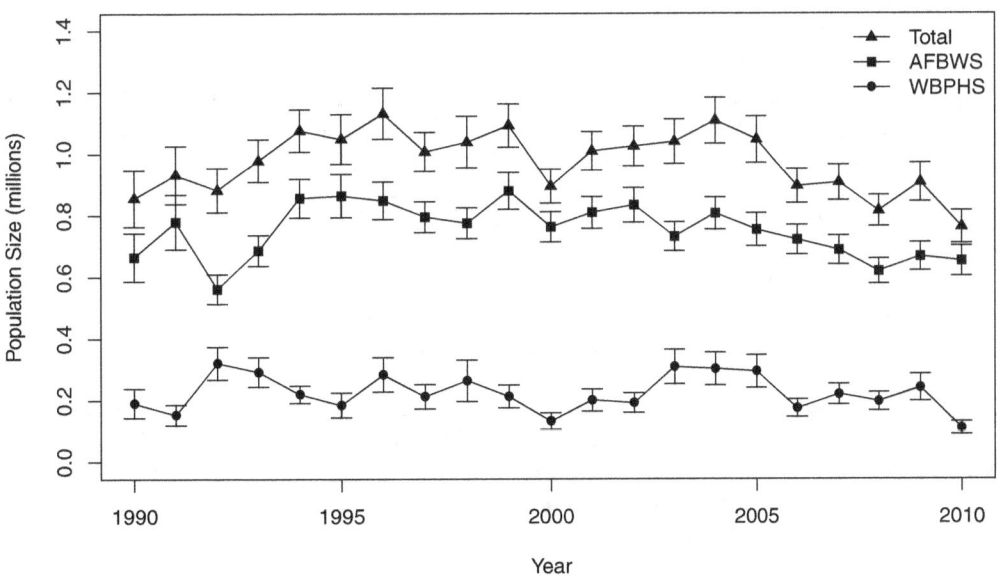

Figure 4 – Population estimates of eastern mallards observed in the northeastern states (AFBWS) and in southern Ontario and Quebec (WBPHS strata 51–54 and 56). Error bars represent one standard error.

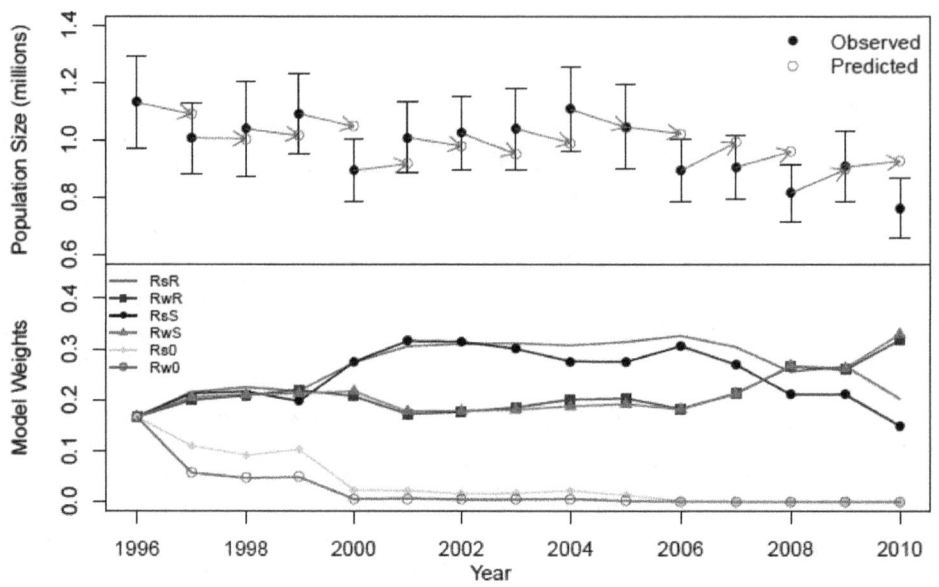

Figure 5 – Top panel: observed population estimates of eastern mallards compared to eastern mallard model set predictions (weighted average based on 2010 model weights) from 1997 to 2010. Error bars represent 95% confidence intervals. Bottom panel: eastern mallard model weights (RsR = strong density-dependent reproduction and biased reproductive rates, RwR = weak density-dependent reproduction and biased reproductive rates, RsS = strong density-dependent reproduction and biased survival rates, RwS = weak density-dependent reproduction and biased survival rates, and Rs0 = strong-dependent reproduction and no model bias, Rw0 = weak density-dependent reproduction and no model bias). Model weights were assumed to be equal in 1996.

4.3 Western Stock

Western mallards consist of 2 substocks and are defined as those birds breeding in Alaska (WBPHS strata 1–12) and those birds breeding in California and Oregon (state surveys; see Figure 1). Estimates of the size of these subpopulations have varied from 0.283 to 0.843 million in Alaska since 1990 and 0.355 to 0.694 million in California and Oregon since 1992 (Table D.1, Figure 6). The total population size of western mallards has ranged from 0.748 to 1.407 million. For 2010, the estimated breeding-population size of western mallards was 1.049 million (SE = 0.077 million), including 0.443 million (SE = 0.056 million) from California and Oregon and 0.606 million (SE = 0.053 million) from Alaska.

Ideally, the western mallard stock assessment would account for mallards breeding in the states of the Pacific Flyway (including Alaska), British Columbia, and the Yukon Territory. However, we have had continuing concerns about our ability to determine changes in population size based on the collection of surveys conducted independently by Pacific Flyway States and the CWS in British Columbia. These surveys tend to vary in design and intensity, and in some cases lack measures of precision. We reviewed extant surveys to determine their adequacy for supporting a western-mallard AHM protocol and selected Alaska, California, and Oregon for modeling purposes. These three states likely harbor about 75% of the western-mallard breeding population. Nonetheless, this geographic delineation is considered temporary until surveys in other areas can be brought up to similar standards and an adequate record of population estimates is available for analysis.

Details concerning the set of population models for western mallards are provided in Appendix D. To predict changes in abundance we relied on a discrete logistic model, which combines reproduction and natural mortality into a single parameter, r, the intrinsic rate of growth. This model assumes density-dependent growth, which is regulated by the ratio of population size, N, to the carrying capacity of the environment,

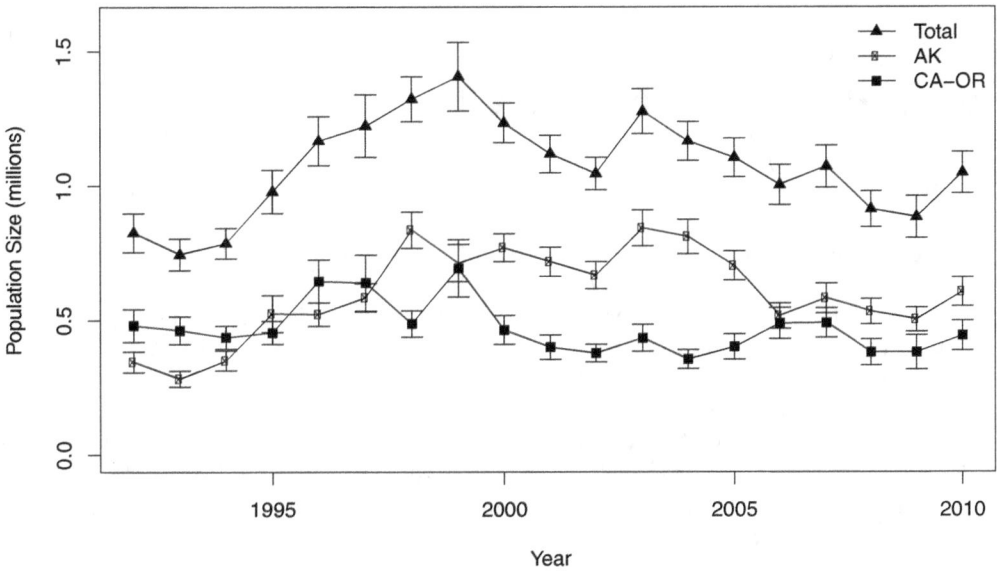

Figure 6 – Population estimates of western mallards observed in Alaska (WBPHS strata 1–12), California and Oregon (state surveys) combined. Error bars represent one standard error.

K (i.e., equilibrium population size in the absence of harvest). In the traditional formulation of the logistic model, harvest mortality is completely additive and any compensation for hunting losses occurs as a result of density-dependent responses beginning in the subsequent breeding season. To increase the model's generality we included a scaling parameter for harvest that allows for the possibility of compensation prior to the breeding season. It is important to note, however, that this parameterization does not incorporate any hypothesized mechanism for harvest compensation and, therefore, must be interpreted cautiously. We modeled Alaska mallards independently of those in California and Oregon because of differing population trajectories (see Figure 6) and substantial differences in the distribution of band recoveries.

We used Bayesian estimation methods in combination with a state-space model that accounts explicitly for both process and observation error in breeding population size (Meyer and Millar 1999). Breeding population estimates of mallards in Alaska are available since 1955, but we had to limit the time series to 1990–2009 because of changes in survey methodology and insufficient band-recovery data. The logistic model and associated posterior parameter estimates provided a reasonable fit to the observed time series of Alaska population estimates. The estimated mean carrying capacity was 1.13 million, the intrinsic rate of growth was 0.31, while the scaling parameter estimate suggests that harvest mortality may be additive. Breeding population and harvest-rate data were available for California and Oregon mallards for the period 1992–2008. The logistic model also provided a reasonable fit to these data, suggesting a mean carrying capacity of 0.64 million, an intrinsic rate of growth of 0.33, while the scaling parameter estimate suggests that harvest mortality may be only partially additive.

Ideally, the development of AHM protocols for mallards would consider how different breeding stocks distribute themselves among the four Flyways so that Flyway-specific harvest strategies could account for the mixing of birds during the hunting season. At present, however, a joint optimization of western, mid-continent, and eastern stocks is not feasible due to computational hurdles. However, our preliminary analyses suggest that the lack of a joint optimization does not result in a significant decrease in performance. Therefore, the AHM protocol for western mallards is structured similarly to that used for eastern mallards, in which an optimal harvest strategy is based on the status of a single breeding stock and harvest regulations in a single flyway. Although the contribution of mid-continent mallards to the Pacific Flyway harvest is significant, we believe an independent harvest strategy for western mallards poses little risk to the mid-continent stock. Further analyses will be needed to confirm this conclusion, and to better understand the potential effect of mid-continent mallard status on sustainable hunting opportunities in the Pacific Flyway.

5 HARVEST-MANAGEMENT OBJECTIVES

The basic harvest-management objective for mid-continent mallards is to maximize cumulative harvest over the long term, which inherently requires perpetuation of a viable population. Moreover, this objective is constrained to avoid regulations that could be expected to result in a subsequent population size below the goal of the North American Waterfowl Management Plan (NAWMP). According to this constraint, the value of harvest decreases proportionally as the difference between the goal and expected population size increases. This balance of harvest and population objectives results in a regulatory strategy that is more conservative than that for maximizing long-term harvest, but more liberal than a strategy to attain the NAWMP goal (regardless of effects on hunting opportunity). The current objective for mid-continent mallards uses a population goal of 8.5 million birds, which consists of 7.9 million mallards from the WBPHS (strata 13–18, 20–50, and 75–77) corresponding to the mallard population goal in the 1998 update of the NAWMP (less the portion of the mallard goal comprised of birds breeding in Alaska) and a goal of 0.6 million for the combined states of Michigan, Minnesota, and Wisconsin.

For eastern and western mallards, there is no NAWMP goal or other established target for desired population size. Accordingly, the management objective for eastern and western mallards is simply to maximize long-term cumulative (i.e., sustainable) harvest. Additionally for western mallards, maximum long-term cumulative harvest is subject to a constraint intended to prevent extreme changes in regulations associated with relatively small changes in population sizes.

6 REGULATORY ALTERNATIVES

6.1 Evolution of Alternatives

When AHM was first implemented in 1995, three regulatory alternatives characterized as liberal, moderate, and restrictive were defined based on regulations used during 1979–84, 1985–87, and 1988–93, respectively. These regulatory alternatives also were considered for the 1996 hunting season. In 1997, the regulatory alternatives were modified to include: (1) the addition of a very-restrictive alternative; (2) additional days and a higher duck bag limit in the moderate and liberal alternatives; and (3) an increase in the bag limit of hen mallards in the moderate and liberal alternatives. In 2002, the USFWS further modified the moderate and liberal alternatives to include extensions of approximately one week in both the opening and closing framework dates.

In 2003, the very-restrictive alternative was eliminated at the request of the Flyway Councils. Expected harvest rates under the very-restrictive alternative did not differ significantly from those under the restrictive alternative, and the very-restrictive alternative was expected to be prescribed for <5% of all hunting seasons. Also in 2003, at the request of the Flyway Councils the USFWS agreed to exclude closed duck-hunting seasons from the AHM protocol when the population size of mid-continent mallards was ≥5.5 million (WBPHS strata 1–18, 20–50, and 75–77 plus the Great Lakes region). Based on our original assessment, closed hunting seasons did not appear to be necessary from the perspective of sustainable harvesting when the mid-continent mallard population exceeded this level. The impact of maintaining open seasons above this level also appeared negligible for other mid-continent duck species, as based on population models developed by Johnson (2003).

In 2008, because of the re-definition of the mid-continent mallard stock that excludes mallards breeding in Alaska, we re-scaled the closed-season constraint. Initially, we attempted to adjust the original 5.5 million

Table 1 – Regulatory alternatives for the 2010 duck-hunting season.

Regulation	Flyway			
	Atlantic[a]	Mississippi	Central[b]	Pacific[c]
Shooting Hours	one-half hour before sunrise to sunset			
Framework Dates				
Restrictive	Oct 1–Jan 20	Saturday nearest Oct 1 to the Sunday nearest Jan 20		
Moderate	Saturday nearest September 24 to the last Sunday in January			
Liberal				
Season Length (days)				
Restrictive	30	60	39	60
Moderate	45	45	60	86
Liberal	60	60	74	107
Bag Limit (total / mallard / hen mallard)				
Restrictive	3 / 3 / 1	3 / 2 / 1	3 / 3 / 1	4 / 3 / 1
Moderate	6 / 4 / 2	6 / 4 / 1	6 / 5 / 1	7 / 5 / 2
Liberal	6 / 4 / 2	6 / 4 / 2	6 / 5 / 2	7 / 7 / 2

[a] The states of Maine, Massachusetts, Connecticut, Pennsylvania, New Jersey, Maryland, Delaware, West Virginia, Virginia, and North Carolina are permitted to exclude Sundays, which are closed to hunting, from their total allotment of season days.

[b] The High Plains Mallard Management Unit is allowed 12, 23, and 23 extra days in the restrictive, moderate, and liberal alternatives, respectively.

[c] The Columbia Basin Mallard Management Unit is allowed seven extra days in the restrictive and moderate alternatives.

closure threshold by subtracting out the 1985 Alaska breeding population estimate, which was the year upon which the original closed season constraint was based. Our initial re-scaling resulted in a new threshold equal to 5.25 million. Simulations based on optimal policies using this revised closed season constraint suggested that the Mississippi and Central Flyways would experience a 70% increase in the frequency of closed seasons. At this time, we agreed to consider alternative re-scalings in order to minimize the effects on the mid-continent mallard strategy and account for the increase in mean breeding population sizes in Alaska over the past several decades. Based on this assessment, we recommended a revised closed season constraint of 4.75 million which resulted in a strategy performance equivalent to the performance expected prior to the re-definition of the mid-continent mallard stock. Because the performance of the revised strategy is essentially unchanged from the original strategy, we believe it will have no greater impact on other duck stocks in the Mississippi and Central Flyways. However, complete- or partial-season closures for particular species or populations could still be deemed necessary in some situations regardless of the status of mid-continent mallards. Details of the regulatory alternatives for each Flyway are provided in Table 1.

6.2 Regulation-Specific Harvest Rates

Harvest rates of mallards associated with each of the open-season regulatory alternatives were initially predicted using harvest-rate estimates from 1979–84, which were adjusted to reflect current hunter numbers and contemporary specifications of season lengths and bag limits. In the case of closed seasons in the U.S., we assumed rates of harvest would be similar to those observed in Canada during 1988–93, which was a period of restrictive regulations both in Canada and the U.S. All harvest-rate predictions were based only in part on band-recovery data, and relied heavily on models of hunting effort and success derived from hunter surveys (Appendix C in U. S. Fish and Wildlife Service 2002). As such, these predictions had large sampling variances and their accuracy was uncertain.

In 2002, we began relying on Bayesian statistical methods for improving regulation-specific predictions of harvest rates, including predictions of the effects of framework-date extensions. Essentially, the idea is to use existing (prior) information to develop initial harvest-rate predictions (as above), to make regulatory decisions based on those predictions, and then to observe realized harvest rates. Those observed harvest rates, in turn, are treated as new sources of information for calculating updated (posterior) predictions. Bayesian methods are attractive because they provide a quantitative, formal, and an intuitive approach to adaptive management.

For mid-continent mallards, we have empirical estimates of harvest rate from the recent period of liberal hunting regulations (1998–2009). The Bayesian methods thus allow us to combine these estimates with our prior predictions to provide updated estimates of harvest rates expected under the liberal regulatory alternative. Moreover, in the absence of experience (so far) with the restrictive and moderate regulatory alternatives, we reasoned that our initial predictions of harvest rates associated with those alternatives should be re-scaled based on a comparison of predicted and observed harvest rates under the liberal regulatory alternative. In other words, if observed harvest rates under the liberal alternative were 10% less than predicted, then we might also expect that the mean harvest rate under the moderate alternative would be 10% less than predicted. The appropriate scaling factors currently are based exclusively on prior beliefs about differences in mean harvest rate among regulatory alternatives, but they will be updated once we have experience with something other than the liberal alternative. A detailed description of the analytical framework for modeling mallard harvest rates is provided in Appendix E.

Our models of regulation-specific harvest rates also allow for the marginal effect of framework-date extensions in the moderate and liberal alternatives. A previous analysis by the U. S. Fish and Wildlife Service (2001) suggested that implementation of framework-date extensions might be expected to increase the harvest rate of mid-continent mallards by about 15%, or in absolute terms by about 0.02 (SD = 0.01). Based on the observed harvest rates during the 2002–2009 hunting seasons, the updated (posterior) estimate of the marginal change in harvest rate attributable to the framework-date extension is 0.007 (SD = 0.007). The estimated effect of the framework-date extension has been to increase harvest rate of mid-continent mallards by about 6% over what would otherwise be expected in the liberal alternative. However, the reader is strongly cautioned that reliable inference about the marginal effect of framework-date extensions ultimately depends on a rigorous experimental design (including controls and random application of treatments).

Current predictions of harvest rates of adult-male mid-continent mallards associated with each of the regulatory alternatives are provided in Table 2. Predictions of harvest rates for the other age and sex cohorts are based on the historical ratios of cohort-specific harvest rates to adult-male rates (Runge et al. 2002). These ratios are considered fixed at their long-term averages and are 1.5407, 0.7191, and 1.1175 for young males, adult females, and young females, respectively. We make the simplifying assumption that the harvest rates of mid-continent mallards depend solely on the regulatory choice in the Mississippi and Central Flyways.

The predicted harvest rates of eastern mallards are updated in the same fashion as that for mid-continent

Table 2 – Predictions of harvest rates of adult-male mid-continent mallards expected with application of the 2010 regulatory alternatives in the Mississippi and Central Flyways.

Regulatory alternative	Mean	SD
Closed (U.S.)	0.0088	0.0019
Restrictive	0.0562	0.0129
Moderate	0.1002	0.0216
Liberal	0.1165	0.0197

mallards based on reward banding conducted in eastern Canada and the northeastern U.S. (Appendix E). Like mid-continent mallards, harvest rates of age and sex cohorts other than adult male mallards are based on constant rates of differential vulnerability as derived from band-recovery data. For eastern mallards, these constants are 1.153, 1.331, and 1.509 for adult females, young males, and young females, respectively (Johnson et al. 2002a). Regulation-specific predictions of harvest rates of adult-male eastern mallards are provided in Table 3.

Table 3 – Predictions of harvest rates of adult-male eastern mallards expected with application of the 2010 regulatory alternatives in the Atlantic Flyway.

Regulatory alternative	Mean	SD
Closed (U.S.)	0.0805	0.0232
Restrictive	0.1103	0.0392
Moderate	0.1361	0.0475
Liberal	0.1476	0.0418

In contrast to mid-continent mallards, framework-date extensions were expected to increase the harvest rate of eastern mallards by only about 5% (U. S. Fish and Wildlife Service 2001), or in absolute terms by about 0.01 (SD = 0.01). Based on the observed harvest rates during the 2002–2009 hunting seasons, the updated (posterior) estimate of the marginal change in harvest rate attributable to the framework-date extension is 0.003 (SD = 0.009). The estimated effect of the framework-date extension has been to increase harvest rate of eastern mallards by about 2% over what would otherwise be expected in the liberal alternative.

Based on available estimates of harvest rates of mallards banded in California and Oregon during 1990–1995 and 2002–2007, there was no apparent relationship between harvest rate and regulatory changes in the Pacific Flyway. This is unusual given our ability to document such a relationship in other mallard stocks and in other species. We note, however, that the period 2002–2007 was comprised of both stable and liberal regulations and harvest rate estimates were based solely on reward bands. Regulations were relatively restrictive during most of the earlier period and harvest rates were estimated based on standard bands using reporting rates estimated from reward banding during 1987–1988. Additionally, 1993–1995 were transition years in which full-address and toll-free bands were being introduced and information to assess their reporting rates (and their effects on reporting rates of standard bands) is limited. Thus, the two periods in which we wish to compare harvest rates are characterized not only by changes in regulations, but also in estimation methods.

Consequently, we lack a sound empirical basis for predicting harvest rates of western mallards associated with current regulatory alternatives in the Pacific Flyway. In 2009, we applied Bayesian statistical methods for improving regulation-specific predictions of harvest rates (see Appendix E). The methodology is analogous to that currently in use for mid-continent and eastern mallards except that the marginal effect of framework date extensions in moderate and liberal alternatives is inestimable because there are no data prior to implementation of extensions. In 2008, we specified prior regulation-specific harvest rates of 0.01, 0.06, 0.09, and 0.11 with associated standard deviations of 0.003, 0.02, 0.03, and 0.03 for the closed, restrictive, moderate, and liberal alternatives, respectively. The harvest rates for the liberal alternative were based on empirical estimates realized under the current liberal alternative during 2002–2007 and determined from adult-male mallards banded with reward bands in California and Oregon. Harvest rates for the moderate and restrictive alternatives were based on the proportional (0.85 and 0.51) difference in harvest rates expected for mid-continent mallards under the respective alternatives. And finally, harvest rate for the closed alternative was based on what we might realize with a closed season in the U.S. (including Alaska) and a very restrictive season in Canada, similar to that for mid-continent mallards. A relatively large standard deviation ($CV = 0.3$) was chosen to reflect greater uncertainty about the means than that for mid-continent mallards ($CV = 0.2$). Current predictions (2010) of harvest rates of adult-male western mallards associated with each regulatory alternative are provided in Table 4.

Table 4 – Predictions of harvest rates of adult-male western mallards expected with application of the 2010 regulatory alternatives in the Pacific Flyway.

Regulatory alternative	Mean	SD
Closed (U.S.)	0.0097	0.0182
Restrictive	0.0592	0.0163
Moderate	0.0984	0.0271
Liberal	0.1149	0.0306

7 OPTIMAL REGULATORY STRATEGIES

We calculated optimal regulatory strategies using stochastic dynamic programming (Lubow 1995, Johnson and Williams 1999). For the Mississippi and Central Flyways, we based this optimization on: (1) the 2010 regulatory alternatives, including the closed-season constraint; (2) current population models and associated weights for mid-continent mallards; and (3) the dual objectives of maximizing long-term cumulative harvest and achieving a population goal of 8.5 million mid-continent mallards. The resulting regulatory strategy (Table 5) is similar to that used last year. Note that prescriptions for closed seasons in this strategy represent resource conditions that are insufficient to support one of the current regulatory alternatives, given current harvest-management objectives and constraints. However, closed seasons under all of these conditions are not necessarily required for long-term resource protection, and simply reflect the NAWMP population goal and the nature of the current regulatory alternatives. Assuming that regulatory choices adhered to this strategy (and that current model weights accurately reflect population dynamics), breeding-population size would be expected to average 6.87 million (SD = 1.86 million). Based on an estimated population size of 8.60 million mid-continent mallards and 3.73 million ponds in Prairie Canada, the optimal choice for the Mississippi and Central Flyways in 2010 is the liberal regulatory alternative.

We calculated an optimal regulatory strategy for the Atlantic Flyway based on: (1) the 2010 regulatory alternatives; (2) current population models and associated weights for eastern mallards; and (3) an objective to maximize long-term cumulative harvest. The resulting strategy suggests liberal regulations for all population sizes of record, and is characterized by a lack of intermediate regulations (Table 6). We simulated the use of this regulatory strategy to determine expected performance characteristics. Assuming that harvest management adhered to this strategy (and that current model weights accurately reflect population dynamics), breeding-population size would be expected to average 0.904 million (SD = 0.184 million). Based on an estimated breeding population size of 0.763 million mallards, the optimal choice for the Atlantic Flyway in 2010 is the liberal regulatory alternative.

We calculated an optimal regulatory strategy for the Pacific Flyway based on: (1) the 2010 regulatory alternatives, (2) current (1990–2009) population models and parameter estimates, and (3) an objective to maximize long-term cumulative harvest subject to a constraint intended to prevent extreme changes in regulations associated with relatively small changes in population sizes (Table 7). We simulated the use of this regulatory strategy to determine expected performance characteristics. Assuming that harvest management adhered to this strategy (and that current model parameters accurately reflect population dynamics), breeding-population size would be expected to average 1.05 million (SD = 0.18 million) in Alaska and 0.45 million (SD = 0.01 million) in California and Oregon. Based on an estimated breeding population size of 0.606 million mallards in Alaska and 0.443 million in California and Oregon, the optimal choice for the Pacific Flyway in 2010 is the liberal regulatory alternative (see Table 7).

Table 5 – Optimal regulatory strategy[a] for the Mississippi and Central Flyways for the 2010 hunting season. This strategy is based on current regulatory alternatives (including the closed-season constraint), mid-continent mallard models and weights, and the dual objectives of maximizing long-term cumulative harvest and achieving a population goal of 8.5 million mallards. The shaded cell indicates the regulatory prescription for 2010.

	Ponds[c]									
Bpop[b]	1.5	2.0	2.5	3.0	3.5	4.0	4.5	5.0	5.5	6.0
≤4.5	C	C	C	C	C	C	C	C	C	C
4.75–5.75	R	R	R	R	R	R	R	R	R	R
6	R	R	R	R	R	R	R	R	M	M
6.25	R	R	R	R	R	R	M	M	M	L
6.5	R	R	R	R	M	M	M	L	L	L
6.75	R	R	R	M	L	L	L	L	L	L
7	R	M	M	M	L	L	L	L	L	L
7.25	M	L	L	L	L	L	L	L	L	L
7.5	L	L	L	L	L	L	L	L	L	L
≥7.75	L	L	L	L	L	L	L	L	L	L

[a] C = closed season, R = restrictive, M = moderate, L = liberal.

[b] Mallard breeding population size (in millions) in the WBPHS (strata 13–18, 20–50, 75–77) and Michigan, Minnesota, and Wisconsin.

[c] Ponds (in millions) in Prairie Canada in May.

Table 6 – Optimal regulatory strategy[a] for the Atlantic Flyway for the 2010 hunting season. This strategy is based on current regulatory alternatives, eastern mallard models and weights, and an objective to maximize long-term cumulative harvest. The shaded cell indicates the regulatory prescription for 2010.

Mallards[b]	Regulation
≤0.350	C
0.375	R
≥0.400	L

[a] C = closed season, R = restrictive, M = moderate, L = liberal.

[b] Estimated number of mallards (in millions) in eastern Canada (WBPHS strata 51–54, 56) and the northeastern U.S. (AFBWS).

8 APPLICATION OF AHM CONCEPTS TO OTHER STOCKS

The USFWS is striving to apply the principles and tools of AHM to improve decision-making for several other stocks of waterfowl. Over the last year, some progress has been made to develop AHM frameworks for American black ducks (*Anas rubripes*) and the Atlantic Population of Canada geese (*Branta canadensis*), but these results are not yet finalized for inclusion in this year's report. As these frameworks are developed further, we will continue to describe this work in subsequent reports. Below, we provide the 2010 updates for two decision-making frameworks that are currently informing harvest management.

Table 7 – Optimal regulatory strategy[a] for the Pacific Flyway during the 2010 hunting season. This strategy is based on the 2010 regulatory alternatives, current (1990–2009) western mallard population models and parameter estimates, and an objective to maximize long-term cumulative harvest subject to a constraint intended to prevent extreme changes in regulations associated with relatively small changes in population sizes. The shaded cell indicates the regulatory prescription for 2010.

CA–OR BPOP[b]	Alaska BPOP[b]											
	0	0.05	0.10	0.15	0.20	0.25	0.30	0.35	0.40	0.45	0.50	≥0.55
0	C	C	L	L	L	L	L	L	L	L	L	L
0.05	C	C	R	R	R	M	M	M	M	L	L	L
0.10	C	R	R	M	M	L	L	L	L	L	L	L
0.15	R	R	M	M	L	L	L	L	L	L	L	L
0.20	M	R	M	L	L	L	L	L	L	L	L	L
0.25	L	R	L	L	L	L	L	L	L	L	L	L
0.30	L	M	L	L	L	L	L	L	L	L	L	L
0.35	L	M	L	L	L	L	L	L	L	L	L	L
0.40	L	M	L	L	L	L	L	L	L	L	L	L
≥0.45	L	M	L	L	L	L	L	L	L	L	L	L

[a] C = closed season, R = restrictive, M = moderate, L = liberal.

[b] Estimated number of mallards (in millions) for Alaska (WBPHS strata 1–12) and in California and Oregon.

8.1 Northern Pintails

Over the past two years, scientists from the U.S. Geological Survey (USGS) and the USFWS, in consultation with the Flyway Councils, have collaborated on the development of an adaptive management framework to inform northern pintail (*Anas acuta*) harvest management. The proposed framework has been revised a number of times in response to comments and feedback from the Flyways. For 2010, the Flyway Councils and the USFWS agreed that the adaptive framework be adopted to inform pintail harvest management decisions. The current, adaptive protocol is based on: (1) an explicit harvest management objective; (2) regulatory alternatives that do not admit partial seasons or 3-bird daily bag limits; (3) a formal optimization process using stochastic dynamic programming (Lubow 1995, Johnson and Williams 1999); (4) harvest allocation on a national rather than Flyway-by-Flyway basis, with no explicit attempt to achieve a particular allocation of harvest among Flyways; and (5) the same system models as the previous prescribed strategy. Details describing the historical development of the technical and policy elements of the 2010 northern pintail harvest strategy can be found in the northern pintail harvest strategy document (U. S. Fish and Wildlife Service 2010).

The harvest-management objective for the northern pintail population is to maximize long term cumulative harvest, which inherently requires perpetuation of a viable population. This objective is specified under a constraint that provides for an open hunting season when the observed breeding population is above 1.75 million birds (based on the lowest observed breeding population size since 1985 of 1.79 million birds in 2002).

The single objective and constraint, in conjunction with the regulatory options (see next section) were determined after an intensive elicitation process with the waterfowl management community. The resulting management objective serves to integrate and balance multiple competing objectives for pintail harvest management, including minimizing closed seasons, eliminating partial seasons (shorter pintail season within the general duck season), maximizing seasons with liberal season length and greater than 1-bird daily bag limit, and minimizing large changes in regulations. These multiple, competing objectives relate directly or indirectly to more fundamental objectives that stakeholders have for pintail harvest management, which may include the following (1) conserve pintail populations indefinitely (a legal requirement under the Migratory Bird Treaty Act); (2) provide harvest opportunity; (3) minimize regulatory burden on the public; (4) encourage hunter participation; and (5) provide for other non-consumptive uses.

The adaptive management protocol considers a range of regulatory alternatives for pintail harvest management that includes a closed season, 1-bird daily bag limit, or 2-bird daily bag limit. The maximum pintail season length depends on the general duck season framework (characterized as liberal, moderate, or restrictive and varying by Flyway) specified by mallard AHM. Each regulatory combination of bag limit and season length has an associated predicted pintail harvest (Table 8). Technical details that describe the models used to predict harvest can be found in Appendix F.

Table 8 – Total pintail harvest expected from the set of regulatory alternatives specified for each Flyway under the northern pintail adaptive harvest management protocol.

Pacific Atlantic	Central Mississippi	Total Harvest
Closed	Closed	67,000
Liberal 1	Closed	278,000
Liberal 1	Restrictive 3	410,000
Liberal 1	Moderate 3	523,000
Liberal 1	Liberal 1	569,000
Liberal 2	Closed	357,000
Liberal 2	Restrictive 3	490,000
Liberal 2	Moderate 3	603,000
Liberal 2	Liberal 2	672,000

An optimal pintail regulation is calculated under the assumption of a liberal mallard season length in all Flyways. However, if the season length of the general duck season determined by mallard AHM is less than liberal in any of the Flyways, then an appropriate pintail daily bag limit would be substituted for that Flyway. Thus, a shorter season length dictated by mallard AHM would result in an equivalent season length for pintails, but with increased bag limit if the expected harvest remained within allowable limits.

Regulatory substitution rules have been developed for the Central and Mississippi Flyways, where the general duck season length is driven by the mid-continent mallard AHM protocol (Table 9). These substitutions were determined by finding a pintail daily bag limit whose expected harvest was less than or equal to that called for under the national recommendation. Thus, if the national pintail harvest strategy called for a liberal 2-bird bag limit, but the mid-continent mallard season length was moderate, the recommended pintail regulation for the Central and Mississippi Flyways would be moderate in length with a 3-bird bag limit. Because season lengths more restrictive than liberal are expected infrequently in the Atlantic and Pacific Flyways under current eastern and western mallard AHM strategies, substitution rules have not yet been developed for these Flyways. If shorter season lengths were called for in the Pacific or Atlantic Flyway, then similar rules would be specified for these flyways and used to identify the appropriate substitution. In all cases, a substitution produces a lower expected harvest than the harvest allowed under the pintail strategy .

The current adaptive protocol considers two population models. Each model represents an alternative hypothesis about the effect of harvest on population dynamics: one in which harvest is additive to natural mortality, and another in which harvest is compensatory to natural mortality. The compensatory model assumes that the mechanism for compensation is density-dependent post-harvest (winter) survival. The models

Table 9 – Substitution rules in the Central and Mississippi Flyways for joint implementation of northern pintail and mallard harvest strategies. The mid-continent mallard AHM strategy stipulates the maximum season length for pintails in the Central and Mississippi Flyways. The substitutions are used when the mid-continent mallard season length is less than liberal. For example, if the pintail strategy calls for a liberal season length with a 2-bird bag, but the mid-continent mallard strategy calls for a restrictive season length, the recommended pintail regulation for the Central and Mississippi Flyways would be restrictive in length with a 3-bird bag limit.

Pintail	Mid-continent mallard AHM season length			
Regulation	Closed	Restrictive	Moderate	Liberal
Closed	Closed	Closed	Closed	Closed
Liberal 1	Closed	Restrictive 3	Moderate 3	Liberal 1
Liberal 2	Closed	Restrictive 3	Moderate 3	Liberal 2

differ only in how they incorporate the winter survival rate. In the additive model, winter survival rate is a constant, whereas winter survival is density-dependent in the compensatory model. A complete description of the model set used to predict pintail population change can be found in Appendix F. Model weights for the pintail model set have been updated annually since 2007 by comparing model predictions with observed survey results. As of 2010, current model weights favor the hypothesis that harvest mortality is additive (60%).

Northern pintail optimal regulatory strategies for the 2010 hunting season were calculated using: (1) pintail harvest-management objectives; (2) the 2010 regulatory alternatives; and (3) current population models and model weights. Based on this year's survey results of 3.51 million birds observed at a mean latitude of 54.4 degrees, the optimal regulatory choice for all four flyways is the liberal regulatory alternative with a 2 bird bag (Table 10).

Table 10 – Northern pintail optimal regulatory strategy[a] for all 4 Flyways for the 2010 hunting season. This strategy is based on current regulatory alternatives (including the closed-season constraint), northern pintail models and weights, and the objective of maximizing long-term cumulative harvest. The shaded cell indicates the regulatory prescription for 2010.

	Mean Latitude[c]								
Bpop[b]	53.0	53.5	54.0	54.5	55.0	55.5	56.0	56.5	57.0
≤ 1.75	C	C	C	C	C	C	C	C	C
1.75–2.5	L1	L1	L1	L1	L1	L1	L1	L1	L1
≥ 2.5	L2	L2	L2	L2	L2	L2	L2	L2	L2

[a] C = closed season, L1 = liberal season with 1 bird bag, L2 = liberal season with 2 bird bag.

[b] Observed northern pintail breeding population size (in millions) from the WBPHS (strata 1–50, 75–77)

[c] Mean Latitude (in degrees).

8.2 Scaup

In 2008, the USFWS implemented a decision-making framework for establishing scaup harvest regulations that was initially proposed in 2007 (Boomer and Johnson 2007). In addition, the USFWS committed to working with the Flyways to develop an alternative scaup population model for inclusion in the current decision-making framework. This model will capture the belief that the scaup population will decline to and stabilize at some lower equilibrium level in response to a declining carrying capacity and that harvest at current levels is completely compensatory. We plan to report on our efforts to develop an alternative model at the 2010 AHM Working Group meeting.

In 2007, the USFWS also outlined methods to facilitate the specification of regulatory alternatives for scaup harvest management (Boomer et al. 2007). We proposed harvest thresholds to be considered under regulatory alternatives based on a simulation of an optimal policy that was derived under an objective to achieve 95% of the long-term cumulative harvest. We used this objective because it results in a strategy less sensitive to small change in population size as compared to a strategy derived under an objective to achieve 100% of long-term cumulative harvest. In addition, the 95% objective allows for some harvest opportunity at relatively low population sizes. We have worked with the Flyways to determine what regulations would achieve the allowable harvest thresholds set forth in Boomer et al. (2007). In 2008 during deliberations over scaup regulatory alternatives, the USFWS also agreed to consider a "hybrid season" option that would be available to all Flyways for the restrictive and moderate alternatives. In 2008, initial Restrictive, Moderate, and Liberal scaup regulatory alternatives were defined and implemented in all four Flyways. Subsequent concerns and dialogue led the USFWS to further clarify criteria associated with the establishment of "hybrid seasons" and to allow additional modifications of the alternatives for each Flyway in 2009. Final scaup regulatory alternatives were adopted for each Flyway in 2009. These alternatives will remain in place for a period of three years and then revisited as the latest harvest information is evaluated.

The USFWS will continue to work with the Flyways to determine acceptable harvest-management objectives and evaluate regulatory alternatives to be used in the evolving decision-making framework for scaup harvest management. Presently, the scaup harvest strategy prescribes optimal harvest levels, not optimal regulatory alternatives. It is important to note that we currently have limited ability to predict expected scaup harvest under the newly-established, Flyway-specific scaup regulatory alternatives. The initial regulatory alternatives adopted for each Flyway were based on relatively crude predictions from harvest models developed in Boomer et al. (2007) or alternative harvest models proposed by the Flyways. As we gain experience with scaup regulatory alternatives, we will refine predicted harvest distributions associated with the Flyway-specific alternatives with the ultimate goal being to use regulatory alternatives, as opposed to harvest, as the control variable in deriving future scaup harvest policies.

The lack of scaup demographic information over a sufficient timeframe and at a continental scale precludes the use of a traditional balance equation to represent scaup population and harvest dynamics. As a result, we used a discrete-time, stochastic, logistic-growth population model to represent changes in scaup abundance, while explicitly accounting for scaling issues associated with the monitoring data. Details describing the modeling and assessment framework that has been developed for scaup can be found in Appendix G and in Boomer and Johnson (2007).

We updated the scaup assessment based on the current model formulation and data extending from 1974 through 2009. As in past analyses, the state space formulation and Bayesian analysis framework provided reasonable fits to the observed breeding population and total harvest estimates with realistic measures of variation. The posterior mean estimate of the intrinsic rate of increase (r) is 0.122 while the posterior mean estimate of the carrying capacity (K) is 8.17 million birds. The posterior mean estimate of the scaling parameter (q) is 0.556, ranging between 0.484 and 0.634 with 95% probability.

We calculated an optimal harvest policy for scaup based on: (1) a control variable of total harvest (U.S. and Canada combined), (2) current population model and updated parameter estimates, and (3) an objective to achieve 95% of the long-term cumulative harvest. We simulated the use of this regulatory strategy to determine expected performance characteristics. Assuming that harvest management adhered to this strategy (and that current model parameters accurately reflect population dynamics), breeding-population size would be expected to average 4.56 million (SD = 0.81 million). With an estimated breeding population size of 4.2 million scaup, the optimal harvest level for scaup is 0.35 million (Table 11). Based on the harvest thresholds specified in Boomer et al. (2007), this year's optimal harvest corresponds to the moderate regulatory alternative.

Table 11 – Optimal scaup harvest levels (observed scale in millions) and corresponding breeding population sizes (in millions). This strategy is based on the current scaup population model, and an objective to maximize 95% of long-term cumulative harvest. The shaded cell indicates the optimal harvest level for 2010 which corresponds to the moderate regulatory alternative.

BPOP	Optimal Harvest
0.0–1.8	0
2.0–2.2	0.05
2.4–2.6	0.10
2.8–3.0	0.15
3.2–3.4	0.20
3.6–3.8	0.25
4.0	0.30
4.2	0.35
4.4	0.40
4.6–4.8	0.45
5.0–5.2	0.50
5.4	0.55

9 EMERGING ISSUES IN AHM

Learning occurs passively with the current AHM protocol as annual comparisons of model predictions to observations from monitoring programs are used to update model weights and relative beliefs about system responses to management (Johnson et al. 2002b) or as model parameters are updated based on an assessment of the most recent monitoring data (Boomer and Johnson 2007, Johnson et al. 2007). However, learning can also occur as decision-making frameworks are evaluated to determine if objectives are being achieved, have changed, or if other aspects of the decision problem are adequately being addressed. Often the feedback resulting from this process results in a form of "double loop" learning (Lee 1993) that offers the opportunity to adapt decision-making frameworks in response to a shifting decision context, novel or emerging management alternatives, or a need to revise models that may perform poorly or need to account for new information. Adaptive management depends on this iterative process to ensure that decision-making protocols remain relevant in evolving biological and social systems.

As a byproduct of the adaptive management process, it is natural to think about when or how decision-making protocols should be revised to incorporate new information or to accommodate changes in the overall management context. Recent outcomes from the 2008 Future of Waterfowl Management Workshop and evaluations of waterfowl harvest and habitat management programs (e.g., Anderson et al. 2007) suggest compelling reasons for a re-evaluation of the objectives of waterfowl management as well as the technical and institutional frameworks through which harvest and habitat management decisions are made. The AHM working group recognizes the need to better integrate harvest and habitat management objectives (sensu Runge et al. 2005, Anderson et al. 2007) as an ongoing effort to continue to make informed decisions while attempting to maximize management efficiency. Within the last year, the waterfowl management community has engaged in an broad-scale effort to determine the fundamental objectives of waterfowl management as part of a structured process to inform the North American Waterfowl Management Plan Revision (North American Waterfowl Management Plan Revision Steering Committee 2009). The results of this consultation and the content of the NAWMP Revision may have significant implications for all of the policy elements currently defined in existing AHM protocols. We view such introspection as completely consistent with the principles underlying AHM, and, in fact, critical to its long-term utility as a decision framework for waterfowl harvest regulation.

The AHM Working Group has also begun discussing the technical challenges involved with dealing with large-scale habitat and environmental change on the decision-making frameworks used to inform waterfowl harvest management. We anticipate that large-scale system change will exacerbate all forms of uncertainty that affect waterfowl AHM, but we believe that the elements of the current AHM framework provide the necessary structure for coping with these changing systems. In addition, the AHM Working Group continues to explore questions related to the appropriate taxonomic, spatial, and temporal resolution of waterfowl harvest management. These, and other issues, are also being considered in the course of ongoing deliberations over the draft 2010 Supplemental Environmental Impact Statement on the Issuance of Annual Regulations Permitting the Hunting of Migratory Birds (U. S. Department of the Interior 2010). In light of these issues, we remain committed to the continued reassessment of AHM decision frameworks through the adaptive process of "double loop" learning. Ultimately, we will need to prioritize the scope of work required to revisit AHM protocols in the face of limited resources, shifting priorities, and in response to rapidly changing biological and social systems. We look forward to working with the Flyways as we continue to refine the adaptive harvest management framework.

LITERATURE CITED

Anderson, D. R., and K. P. Burnham, 1976. Populatin ecology of the mallard. VI. The effect of exploitation on survival. U. S. Fish and Wildlife Service Resource Publication. 128. 66pp.

Anderson, M. G., D. Casewell, J. M. Eadie, J. T. Herbert, M. Huang, D. D. Humberg, F. A. Johnson, M. D. Koneff, S. E. Mott, T. D. Nudds, E. T. Reed, J. K. Ringleman, M. C. Runge, and B. C. Wilson, 2007. Unpublished Report from the Joint Task Group for clarifying North American waterfowl management plan population objectives and their use in harvest management.

Blohm, R. J. 1989. Introduction to harvest – understanding surveys and season setting. Proceedings of the International Waterfowl Symposium 6:118–133.

Blohm, R. J., R. E. Reynolds, J. P. Bladen, J. D. Nichols, J. E. Hines, K. P. Pollock, and R. T. Eberhardt. 1987. Mallard mortality rates on key breeding and wintering areas. Transactions of the North American Wildilfe and Resources Conference 52:246–263.

Boomer, G. S., and F. A. Johnson, 2007. A proposed assessment and decision-making framework to inform scaup harvest management. Unpublished Report. U. S. Fish and Wildlife Service, Laurel, MD. 26pp., URL http://www.fws.gov/migratorybirds/NewReportsPublications/SpecialTopics/BySpecies/SCAUP2007Report.pdf.

Boomer, G. S., F. A. Johnson, M. D. Koneff, T. A. Sanders, and R. E. Trost, 2007. A process to determine scaup regulatory alternatives. Unpublished Scoping Document. U. S. Fish and Wildlife Service, Laurel, MD. 20pp., URL http://www.fws.gov/migratorybirds/NewReportsPublications/SpecialTopics/BySpecies/scaup_regs_scoping_draftVI.pdf.

Brooks, S. P., and A. Gelman. 1998. Alternative methods for monitoring convergence of iterative simulations. Journal of Computational and Graphical Statistics 7:434–455.

Burnham, K. P., G. C. White, and D. R. Anderson. 1984. Estimating the effect of hunting on annual survival rates of adult mallards. Journal of Wildlife Management 48:350–361.

Henny, C. J., and K. P. Burnham. 1976. A reward band study of mallards to estimate reporting rates. Journal of Wildlife Management 40:1–14.

Heusmann, H. W., and J. R. Sauer. 2000. The northeastern states' waterfowl breeding population survey. Wildlife Society Bulletin 28:355–364.

Hodges, J. L., J. G. King, B. Conant, and H. A. Hanson. 1996. Aerial surveys of waterbirds in Alaska 1975–94: population trends and observer variability. National Biological Service, U.S. Department of the Interior Information and Technology Report 4, Washington, D. C.

Johnson, F. A., 2003. Population dynamics of ducks other than mallards in mid-continent North America. Draft. U. S. Fish and Wildlife Service, U. S. Department of the Interior, Washington, D. C. 15pp.

Johnson, F. A., G. S. Boomer, and T. A. Sanders, 2007. A proposed protocol for the adaptive harvest management of mallards breeding in Western North America. Unpublished Report. U. S. Fish and Wildlife Service, Laurel, MD. 33pp.

Johnson, F. A., J. A. Dubovsky, M. C. Runge, and D. R. Eggeman. 2002a. A revised protocol for the adaptive harvest management of eastern mallards. Fish and Wildlife Service, U. S. Department of the Interior Technical report, Washington, D. C. URL http://www.fws.gov/migratorybirds/NewReportsPublications/AHM/Year2002/emal-ahm-2002.pdf.

Johnson, F. A., W. L. Kendall, and J. A. Dubovsky. 2002b. Conditions and limitations on learning in the adaptive management of mallard harvests. Wildlife Society Bulletin 30:176–185.

Johnson, F. A., C. T. Moore, W. L. Kendall, J. A. Dubovsky, D. F. Caithamer, J. Kelley, J. R., and B. K. Williams. 1997. Uncertainty and the management of mallard harvests. Journal of Wildlife Management 61:202–216.

Johnson, F. A., and B. K. Williams. 1999. Protocol and practice in the adaptive management of waterfowl harvests. Conservation Ecology 3:8. URL http://www.consecol.org/vol3/iss1/art8.

Johnson, F. A., B. K. Williams, J. D. Nichols, J. E. Hines, W. L. Kendall, G. W. Smith, and D. F. Caithamer. 1993. Developing an adaptive management strategy for harvesting waterfowl in North America. Transactions of the North American Wildlife and Natural Resources Conference 58:565–583.

Johnson, F. A., B. K. Williams, and P. R. Schmidt. 1996. Adaptive decision-making in waterfowl harvest and habitat management. Proceedings of the International Waterfowl Symposium 7:26–33.

Lee, K. N. 1993. Compass and Gyroscope: Integrating Science and Politics for the Environment. Island Press, Washington, D.C.

Lubow, B. C. 1995. SDP: Generalized software for solving stochastic dynamic optimization problems. Wildlife Society Bulletin 23:738–742.

Meyer, R., and R. B. Millar. 1999. BUGS in Bayesian stock assessments. Canadian Journal of Fisheries and Aquatic Sciences 56:10078–1086.

Millar, R. B., and R. Meyer. 2000. Non-linear state space modeling of fisheries biomass dynamics by using Metropolis-Hastings within Gibbs sampling. Applied Statistics 49:327–342.

Nichols, J. D., F. A. Johnson, and B. K. Williams. 1995a. Managing North American waterfowl in the face of uncertainty. Annual Review of Ecology and Systematics 26:177–199.

Nichols, J. D., R. E. Reynolds, R. J. Blohm, R. E. Trost, J. E. Hines, and J. P. Bladen. 1995b. Geographic variation in band reporting rates for mallards based on reward banding. Journal of Wildlife Management 59:697–708.

North American Waterfowl Management Plan Revision Steering Committee, 2009. North American Waterfowl Management Plan Revision Communiqué. URL http://nawmprevision.org/sites/default/files/Plan_Revision_Communique.pdf.

Runge, M. C., 2007. Northern pintail harvest strategy: development of a compensatory model. Unpublished Report. U. S. Geological Survey, Patuxent Wildlife Research Center, Laurel, MD.

Runge, M. C., and G. S. Boomer, 2005. Population dynamics and harvest management of the continental northern pintail population. Unpublished Report. U. S. Geological Survey, Patuxent Wildlife Research Center, Laurel, MD. 42pp., URL http://www.fws.gov/migratorybirds/NewReportsPublications/AHM/Year2005/NOPI%202005%20Report%202.pdf.

Runge, M. C., F. A. Johnson, M. G. Anderson, M. D. Koneff, E. T. Reed, and S. E. Mott. 2005. The need for coherence between waterfowl harvest and habitat management. Wildlife Society Bulletin 34:1231–1237.

Runge, M. C., F. A. Johnson, J. A. Dubovsky, W. L. Kendall, J. Lawrence, and J. Gammonley. 2002. A revised protocol for the adaptive harvest management of mid-continent mallards. Fish and Wildlife Service, U. S. Department of the Interior Technical report, Washington, D. C. URL http://www.fws.gov/migratorybirds/NewReportsPublications/AHM/Year2002/MCMrevise2002.pdf.

Schaefer, M. B. 1954. Some aspects of the dynamics of populations important to the management of commercial marine fisheries. Bulletin of the Inter-American Tropical Tuna Commission 1:25–56.

Smith, G. W. 1995. A critical review of the aerial and ground surveys of breeding waterfowl in North America. National Biological Service, U. S. Department of the Interior Biological Science Report 5, Washington, D. C.

Spiegelhalter, D. J., A. Thomas, N. Best, and D. Lunn. 2003. WinBUGS 1.4 User manual. MRC Biostatistics Unit, Institues of Public Health, Cambridge, UK.

U. S. Department of the Interior, 2010. Draft Supplemental Environmental Impact Statement: Issuance of Annual Regulations Permitting the Hunting of Migratory Birds. U. S. Fish and Wildlife Service, Washington, D. C. 305pp., URL http://www.fws.gov/migratorybirds/NewReportsPublications/Hunting/SEIS%207%20June%20b%202010.pdf.

U. S. Fish and Wildlife Service, 2000. Adaptive harvest management: 2000 duck hunting season. U. S. Department of Interior, Washington, D. C. 43pp., URL http://www.fws.gov/migratorybirds/NewReportsPublications/AHM/Year2000/ahm2000.pdf.

U. S. Fish and Wildlife Service, 2001. Framework-date extensions for duck hunting in the United States: projected impacts & coping with uncertainty. U. S. Department of Interior, Washington, D. C. 8pp., URL http://www.fws.gov/migratorybirds/NewReportsPublications/AHM/Year2001/ahm2001.pdf.

U. S. Fish and Wildlife Service, 2002. Adaptive harvest management: 2002 duck hunting season. U. S. Department of Interior, Washington, D. C. 34pp., URL http://www.fws.gov/migratorybirds/NewReportsPublications/AHM/Year2002/2002-AHM-report.pdf.

U. S. Fish and Wildlife Service, 2010. Northern Pintail Harvest Strategy. U. S. Department of Interior, Washington, D. C. 20pp., URL http://www.fws.gov/migratorybirds/NewsPublicationsReports.html.

Walters, C. 1986. Adaptive Management of Renewable Resources. Macmillian, New York.

Williams, B. K., and F. A. Johnson. 1995. Adaptive management and the regulation of waterfowl harvests. Wildlife Society Bulletin 23:430–436.

Williams, B. K., F. A. Johnson, and K. Wilkins. 1996. Uncertainty and the adaptive management of waterfowl harvests. Journal of Wildlife Management 60:223–232.

A   AHM WORKING GROUP

(Note: This list includes only permanent members of the AHM Working Group. Not listed here are numerous persons from federal and state agencies that assist the Working Group on an ad-hoc basis.)

Coordinator:

Scott Boomer
U. S. Fish & Wildlife Service
11510 American Holly Drive
Laurel, Maryland 20708-4017
phone: 301-497-5684
fax: 301-497-5871
e-mail: scott_boomer@fws.gov

USFWS Representatives:

Brad Bortner (Region 1)
U. S. Fish & Wildlife Service
911 NE 11th Ave.
Portland, OR 97232-4181
phone: 503-231-6164
fax: 503-231-2364
e-mail: brad_bortner@fws.gov

Dave Case (contractor)
D. J. Case & Associates
607 Lincolnway West
Mishawaka, IN 46544
phone: 574-258-0100
fax: 574-258-0189
e-mail: dave@djcase.com

Jim Dubovsky (Region 6)
U. S. Fish & Wildlife Service
P.O. Box 25486-DFC
Denver, CO 80225-0486
phone: 303-236-4403
fax: 303-236-8680
e-mail: james_dubovsky@fws.gov

Jim Kelley (Region 9)
U. S. Fish & Wildlife Service
1 Federal Drive
Fort Snelling, MN 55111-0458
phone: 612-713-5409
fax: 612-713-5393
e-mail: james_r_kelley@fws.gov

Sean Kelly (Region 3)
U. S. Fish & Wildlife Service
1 Federal Drive
Fort Snelling, MN 55111-4056
phone: 612-713-5470
fax: 612-713-5393
e-mail: sean_kelly@fws.gov

Mark Koneff (Region 9)
U. S. Fish & Wildlife Service
11510 American Holly Drive
Laurel, Maryland 20708-4017
phone: 301-497-5648
fax: 301-497-5871
e-mail: mark_koneff@fws.gov

Jeff Haskins (Region 2)
U. S. Fish & Wildlife Service
P.O. Box 1306
Albuquerque, NM 87103
phone: 505-248-6827 (ext 30)
fax: 505-248-7885
e-mail: jeff_haskins@fws.gov

Diane Pence (Region 5)
U. S. Fish & Wildlife Service
300 Westgate Center Drive
Hadley, MA 01035-9589
phone: 413-253-8577
fax: 413-253-8424
e-mail: diane_pence@fws.gov

Russ Oates (Region 7)
U. S. Fish & Wildlife Service
1011 East Tudor Road
Anchorage, AK 99503-6119
phone: 907-786-3446
fax: 907-786-3641
e-mail: russ_oates@fws.gov

Dave Sharp (Region 9)
U. S. Fish & Wildlife Service
P.O. Box 25486, DFC
Denver, CO 80225-0486
phone: 303-275-2386
fax: 303-275-2384
e-mail: dave_sharp@fws.gov

Paul Padding (Region 9)
U. S. Fish & Wildlife Service
11510 American Holly Drive
Laurel, MD 20708
phone: 301-497-5851
fax: 301-497-5885
e-mail: paul_padding@fws.gov

Bob Trost (Region 9)
U. S. Fish & Wildlife Service
911 NE 11th Ave.
Portland, OR 97232-4181
phone: 503-231-6162
fax: 503-231-6228
e-mail: robert_trost@fws.gov

David Viker (Region 4)
U. S. Fish & Wildlife Service
1875 Century Blvd., Suite 345
Atlanta, GA 30345
phone: 404-679-7188
fax: 404-679-7285
e-mail: david_viker@fws.gov

Canadian Wildlife Service Representatives:

Eric Reed
Canadian Wildlife Service
351 St. Joseph Boulevard
Hull, QC K1A OH3, Canada
phone: 819-953-0294
fax: 819-953-6283
e-mail: eric.reed@ec.gc.ca

Flyway Council Representatives:

Min Huang (Atlantic Flyway)
CT Dept. of Environmental Protection
Franklin Wildlife Mgmt. Area
391 Route 32
North Franklin, CT 06254, USA
Phone: 860-642-6528
fax: 860-642-7964
e-mail: min.huang@po.state.ct.us

Mike Johnson (Central Flyway)
North Dakota Game and Fish Department
100 North Bismarck Expressway
Bismarck, ND 58501-5095
phone: 701-328-6319
fax: 701-328-6352
e-mail: mjohnson@state.nd.us

Bryan Swift (Atlantic Flyway)
NY Dept. Environmental Conservation
625 Broadway
Albany, NY 12233-4754
phone: 518-402-8866
fax: 518-402-9027 or 402-8925
e-mail: blswift@gw.dec.state.ny.us

Mark Vrtiska (Central Flyway)
Nebraska Game and Parks Commission
P.O. Box 30370
2200 North 33rd Street
Lincoln, NE 68503-1417
phone: 402-471-5437
fax: 402-471-5528
email: mvrtiska@ngpc.state.ne.us

Larry Reynolds (Mississippi Flyway)
LA Dept. of Wildlife & Fisheries
P.O. Box 98000
Baton Rouge, LA 70898-9000, USA
Phone: 225-765-0456
Fax: 225-763-5456
e-mail: lreynolds@wlf.state.la.us

Jon Runge (Pacific Flyway)
Colorado Division of Wildlife
317 West Prospect
Fort Collins, CO 80526
Phone: 970-472-4365
e-mail: Jon.Runge@state.co.us

Dan Yparraguirre (Pacific Flyway)
California Dept. of Fish and Game
1812 Ninth Street
Sacramento, CA 95814
phone: 916-445-3685
e-mail: dyparraguirre@dfg.ca.gov

Guy Zenner (Mississippi Flyway)
Iowa Dept. of Natural Resources
1203 North Shore Drive
Clear Lake, IA 50428
phone: 515-357-3517, ext. 23
fax: 515-357-5523
e-mail: gzenner@netins.net

USGS Technical Consultants:

Fred Johnson
Florida Integrated Science Center
U. S. Geological Survey
P.O. Box 110485
Gainesville, FL 32611
phone: 352-392-5075
fax: 352-846-0841
e-mail: fjohnson@usgs.gov

Andy Royle
Patuxent Wildlife Research Center
U. S. Geological Survey
12100 Beech Forest Rd.
Laurel, MD 20708
phone: 301-497-5846
fax: 301-497-5545
e-mail: aroyle@usgs.gov

Mike Runge Patuxent Wildlife Research Center
U. S. Geological Survey
12100 Beech Forest Rd.
Laurel, MD 20708
phone: 301-497-5748
fax: 301-497-5545
e-mail: mrunge@usgs.gov

B   MID-CONTINENT MALLARD MODELS

In 1995, we developed population models to predict changes in mid-continent mallards based on the traditional survey area which includes individuals from Alaska (Johnson et al. 1997). In 1997, we added mallards from the Great Lakes region (Michigan, Minnesota, and Wisconsin) to the mid-continent mallard stock, assuming their population dynamics were equivalent. In 2002, we made extensive revisions to the set of alternative models describing the population dynamics of mid-continent mallards (Runge et al. 2002, U. S. Fish and Wildlife Service 2002). In 2008, we redefined the population of mid-continent mallards (Table 1) to account for the removal of Alaskan birds (WBPHS strata 1–12) that are now considered to be in the western mallard stock and have subsequently rescaled the model set appropriately.

Mid-continent Mallard Breeding Population Estimates

Table B.1 – Estimates (N) and associated standard errors (SE) of mid-continent mallards (in millions) observed in the WBPHS (strata 13–18, 20–50, and 75–77) and the Great Lakes region (Michigan, Minnesota, and Wisconsin).

Year	WBPHS area N	WBPHS area SE	Great Lakes region N	Great Lakes region SE	Total N	Total SE
1992	5.6304	0.2379	0.9946	0.1597	6.6249	0.2865
1993	5.4253	0.2068	0.9347	0.1457	6.3600	0.2529
1994	6.6292	0.2803	1.1505	0.1163	7.7797	0.3035
1995	7.7452	0.2793	1.1214	0.1965	8.8666	0.3415
1996	7.4193	0.2593	1.0251	0.1443	8.4444	0.2967
1997	9.3554	0.3041	1.0777	0.1445	10.4331	0.3367
1998	8.8041	0.294	1.1224	0.1792	9.9266	0.3443
1999	10.0926	0.3374	1.0591	0.2122	11.1518	0.3986
2000	8.6999	0.2855	1.2350	0.1761	9.9348	0.3354
2001	7.1857	0.2204	0.8622	0.1086	8.0479	0.2457
2002	6.8364	0.2412	1.0820	0.1152	7.9184	0.2673
2003	7.1062	0.2589	0.8360	0.0734	7.9422	0.2691
2004	6.6142	0.2746	0.9333	0.0748	7.5474	0.2847
2005	6.0521	0.2754	0.7862	0.0650	6.8383	0.2830
2006	6.7607	0.2187	0.5881	0.0465	7.3488	0.2236
2007	7.7258	0.2805	0.7677	0.0584	8.4935	0.2865
2008	7.1914	0.2525	0.6750	0.0478	7.8664	0.2570
2009	8.0094	0.2442	0.6958	0.0564	8.7052	0.2506
2010	7.8246	0.2799	0.7800	0.0588	8.6046	0.2860

Model Structure

Collectively, the models express uncertainty (or disagreement) about whether harvest is an additive or compensatory form of mortality (Burnham et al. 1984), and whether the reproductive process is weakly or strongly density-dependent (i.e., the degree to which reproductive rates decline with increasing population size).

All population models for mid-continent mallards share a common "balance equation" to predict changes in breeding-population size as a function of annual survival and reproductive rates:

$$N_{t+1} = N_t \left(mS_{t,AM} + (1 - m)(S_{t,AF} + R_t(S_{t,JF} + S_{t,JM}\phi_F^{sum}/\phi_M^{sum})) \right)$$

where:

N = breeding population size,

m = proportion of males in the breeding population,

S_{AM}, S_{AF}, S_{JF}, and S_{JM} = survival rates of adult males, adult females, young females, and young males, respectively,

R = reproductive rate, defined as the fall age ratio of females,

$\phi_F^{sum}/\phi_M^{sum}$ = the ratio of female (F) to male (M) summer survival, and t = year.

We assumed that m and $\phi_F^{sum}/\phi_M^{sum}$ are fixed and known. We also assumed, based in part on information provided by Blohm et al. (1987), the ratio of female to male summer survival was equivalent to the ratio of annual survival rates in the absence of harvest. Based on this assumption, we estimated $\phi_F^{sum}/\phi_M^{sum} = 0.897$. To estimate m we expressed the balance equation in matrix form:

$$\begin{bmatrix} N_{t+1,AM} \\ N_{t+1,AF} \end{bmatrix} = \begin{bmatrix} S_{AM} & RS_{JM}\phi_F^{sum}/\phi_M^{sum} \\ 0 & S_{AF} + R_{JF} \end{bmatrix} \begin{bmatrix} N_{t,AM} \\ N_{t,AF} \end{bmatrix}$$

and substituted the constant ratio of summer survival and means of estimated survival and reproductive rates. The right eigenvector of the transition matrix is the stable sex structure that the breeding population eventually would attain with these constant demographic rates. This eigenvector yielded an estimate of $m = 0.5246$.

Using estimates of annual survival and reproductive rates, the balance equation for mid-continent mallards over-predicted observed population sizes by 11.0% on average. The source of the bias is unknown, so we modified the balance equation to eliminate the bias by adjusting both survival and reproductive rates:

$$N_{t+1} = \gamma_S N_t \left(mS_{t,am} + (1 - m)\left(S_{t,AF} + \gamma_R R_t \left(S_{t,JF} + S_{t,JM}\phi_F^{sum}/\phi_M^{sum}\right)\right)\right)$$

where γ denotes the bias-correction factors for survival (S), and reproduction (R). We used a least squares approach to estimate $\gamma_S = 0.9407$ and $\gamma_R = 0.8647$.

Survival Process

We considered two alternative hypotheses for the relationship between annual survival and harvest rates. For both models, we assumed that survival in the absence of harvest was the same for adults and young of the same sex. In the model where harvest mortality is additive to natural mortality:

$$S_{t,sex,age} = S_{0,sex}^A(1 - K_{t,sex,age})$$

and in the model where changes in natural mortality compensate for harvest losses (up to some threshold):

$$
S_{t,sex,age} = \begin{cases} s_{0,sex}^{C} & if\ K_{t,sex,age} \leq 1 - s_{0,sex}^{C} \\ 1 - K_{t,sex,age} & if\ K_{t,sex,age} > 1 - s_{0,sex}^{C} \end{cases}
$$

where s_0 = survival in the absence of harvest under the additive (A) or compensatory (C) model, and K = harvest rate adjusted for crippling loss (20%, Anderson and Burnham 1976). We averaged estimates of s_0 across banding reference areas by weighting by breeding-population size. For the additive model, $s_0 = 0.7896$ and 0.6886 for males and females, respectively. For the compensatory model, $s_0 = 0.6467$ and 0.5965 for males and females, respectively. These estimates may seem counterintuitive because survival in the absence of harvest should be the same for both models. However, estimating a common (but still sex-specific) s_0 for both models leads to alternative models that do not fit available band-recovery data equally well. More importantly, it suggests that the greatest uncertainty about survival rates is when harvest rate is within the realm of experience. By allowing s_0 to differ between additive and compensatory models, we acknowledge that the greatest uncertainty about survival rate is its value in the absence of harvest (i.e., where we have no experience).

Reproductive Process

Annual reproductive rates were estimated from age ratios in the harvest of females, corrected using a constant estimate of differential vulnerability. Predictor variables were the number of ponds in May in Prairie Canada (P, in millions) and the size of the breeding population (N, in millions). We estimated the best-fitting linear model, and then calculated the 80% confidence ellipsoid for all model parameters. We chose the two points on this ellipsoid with the largest and smallest values for the effect of breeding-population size, and generated a weakly density-dependent model:

$$
R_t = 0.7166 + 0.1083P_t - 0.0373N_t
$$

and a strongly density-dependent model:

$$
R_t = 1.1390 + 0.1376P_t - 0.1131N_t
$$

Predicted recruitment was then rescaled to reflect the current definition of mid-continent mallards which now excludes birds from Alaska but includes mallards observed in the Great Lakes region.

Pond Dynamics

We modeled annual variation in Canadian pond numbers as a first-order autoregressive process. The estimated model was:

$$
P_{t+1} = 2.2127 + 0.3420P_t + \varepsilon_t
$$

where ponds are in millions and ε_t is normally distributed with mean = 0 and variance = 1.2567.

Variance of Prediction Errors

Using the balance equation and sub-models described above, predictions of breeding-population size in year $t+1$ depend only on specification of population size, pond numbers, and harvest rate in year t. For the period in which comparisons were possible, we compared these predictions with observed population sizes.

We estimated the prediction-error variance by setting:

$$e_t = \ln\left(N_t^{obs}\right) - \ln\left(N_t^{pre}\right)$$
$$e_t \sim N\left(0, \sigma^2\right)$$
$$\hat{\sigma^2} = \sum_t \left[\ln\left(N_t^{obs}\right) - \ln\left(N_t^{pre}\right)\right]^2 / (n-1)$$

where N^{obs} and N^{pre} are observed and predicted population sizes (in millions), respectively, and $n =$ the number of years being compared. We were concerned about a variance estimate that was too small, either by chance or because the number of years in which comparisons were possible was small. Therefore, we calculated the upper 80% confidence limit for σ^2 based on a Chi-squared distribution for each combination of the alternative survival and reproductive sub-models, and then averaged them. The final estimate of σ^2 was 0.0280, equivalent to a coefficient of variation of about 18%.

Model Implications

The population model with additive hunting mortality and weakly density-dependent recruitment (SaRw) leads to the most conservative harvest strategy, whereas the model with compensatory hunting mortality and strongly density-dependent recruitment (ScRs) leads to the most liberal strategy. The other two models (SaRs and ScRw) lead to strategies that are intermediate between these extremes. Under the models with compensatory hunting mortality (ScRs and ScRw), the optimal strategy is to have a liberal regulation regardless of population size or number of ponds because at harvest rates achieved under the liberal alternative, harvest has no effect on population size. Under the strongly density-dependent model (ScRs), the density dependence regulates the population and keeps it within narrow bounds. Under the weakly density dependent model (ScRw), the density-dependence does not exert as strong a regulatory effect, and the population size fluctuates more.

Model Weights

Model weights are calculated as Bayesian probabilities, reflecting the relative ability of the individual alternative models to predict observed changes in population size. The Bayesian probability for each model is a function of the models previous (or prior) weight and the likelihood of the observed population size under that model. We used Bayes' theorem to calculate model weights from a comparison of predicted and observed population sizes for the years 1996–2010, starting with equal model weights in 1995.

C EASTERN MALLARD MODELS

We also revised the population models for eastern mallards in 2002 (Johnson et al. 2002a, U. S. Fish and Wildlife Service 2002). The current set of six models: (1) relies solely on federal and state waterfowl surveys (rather than the Breeding Bird Survey) to estimate abundance; (2) allows for the possibility of a positive bias in estimates of survival or reproductive rates; (3) incorporates competing hypotheses of strongly and weakly density-dependent reproduction; and (4) assumes that hunting mortality is additive to other sources of mortality.

Eastern Mallard Breeding Population Estimates

Table C.1 – Estimates (N) and associated standard errors (SE) of eastern mallards (in millions) observed in the northeastern U.S. (AFBWS) and southern Ontario and Quebec (WBPHS strata 51–54 and 56).

Year	Northeastern U.S. N	SE	WBPHS N	SE	Total N	SE
1990	0.6651	0.0783	0.1907	0.0472	0.8558	0.0914
1991	0.7792	0.0883	0.1528	0.0337	0.9320	0.0945
1992	0.5622	0.0479	0.3203	0.0530	0.8825	0.0715
1993	0.6866	0.0499	0.2921	0.0482	0.9786	0.0694
1994	0.8563	0.0628	0.2195	0.0282	1.0758	0.0688
1995	0.8641	0.0704	0.1844	0.0400	1.0486	0.0810
1996	0.8486	0.0611	0.2831	0.0557	1.1317	0.0826
1997	0.7952	0.0496	0.2121	0.0396	1.0073	0.0634
1998	0.7752	0.0497	0.2638	0.0672	1.0390	0.0836
1999	0.8800	0.0602	0.2125	0.0369	1.0924	0.0706
2000	0.7626	0.0487	0.1323	0.0264	0.8948	0.0554
2001	0.8094	0.0516	0.2002	0.0356	1.0097	0.0627
2002	0.8335	0.0562	0.1915	0.0319	1.0250	0.0647
2003	0.7319	0.0470	0.3083	0.0554	1.0402	0.0726
2004	0.8066	0.0517	0.3015	0.0533	1.1081	0.0743
2005	0.7536	0.0536	0.2934	0.0531	1.0470	0.0755
2006	0.7214	0.0476	0.1740	0.0284	0.8954	0.0555
2007	0.6876	0.0467	0.2193	0.0336	0.9069	0.0576
2008	0.6191	0.0407	0.1960	0.0300	0.8151	0.0505
2009	0.6668	0.0457	0.2411	0.0434	0.9078	0.0630
2010	0.6526	0.0492	0.1100	0.0205	0.7626	0.0533

Model Structure

As with mid-continent mallards, all population models for eastern mallards share a common balance equation to predict changes in breeding-population size as a function of annual survival and reproductive rates:

$$N_{t+1} = N_t \left((pS_t^{am}) + \left((1-p)\, S_t^{af} \right) + (p\,(A_t^m/d)\, S_t^{ym}) + \left(p\,(A_t^m/d)\, \psi S_t^{yf} \right) \right)$$

where:

N = breeding-population size,

p = proportion of males in the breeding population,

S^{am}, S^{af}, S^{ym}, and S^{yf} = survival rates of adult males, adult females, young males, and young females, respectively,

A^m = ratio of young males to adult males in the harvest,

d = ratio of young male to adult male direct recovery rates,

ψ = the ratio of male to female summer survival, and t = year.

In this balance equation, we assume that p, d, and ψ are fixed and known. The parameter ψ is necessary to account for the difference in anniversary date between the breeding-population survey (May) and the survival and reproductive rate estimates (August). This model also assumes that the sex ratio of fledged young is 1:1; hence A^m/d appears twice in the balance equation. We estimated $d = 1.043$ as the median ratio of young:adult male band-recovery rates in those states from which wing receipts were obtained. We estimated $\psi = 1.216$ by regressing through the origin estimates of male survival against female survival in the absence of harvest, assuming that differences in natural mortality between males and females occur principally in summer. To estimate p, we used a population projection matrix of the form:

$$\begin{bmatrix} M_{t+1} \\ F_{t+1} \end{bmatrix} = \begin{bmatrix} S^{am} + (A^m/d)\, S^{ym} & 0 \\ (A^m/d)\, \psi S^{yf} & S^{af} \end{bmatrix} \begin{bmatrix} M_t \\ F_t \end{bmatrix}$$

where M and F are the relative number of males and females in the breeding populations, respectively. To parameterize the projection matrix we used average annual survival rate and age ratio estimates, and the estimates of d and ψ provided above. The right eigenvector of the projection matrix is the stable proportion of males and females the breeding population eventually would attain in the face of constant demographic rates. This eigenvector yielded an estimate of $p = 0.544$.

We also attempted to determine whether estimates of survival and reproductive rates were unbiased. We relied on the balance equation provided above, except that we included additional parameters to correct for any bias that might exist. Because we were unsure of the source(s) of potential bias, we alternatively assumed that any bias resided solely in survival rates:

$$N_{t+1} = N_t \omega \left(pS_t^{am} + \left((1-p)\, S_t^{af} \right) + (p\,(A_t^m/d)\, S_t^{ym}) + \left(p\,(A_t^m/d)\, \psi S_t^{yf} \right) \right)$$

(where ω is the bias-correction factor for survival rates), or solely in reproductive rates:

$$N_{t+1} = N_t \left(pS_t^{am} + \left((1-p)\, S_t^{af} \right) + (p\alpha\,(A_t^m/d)\, S_t^{ym}) + \left(p\alpha\,(A_t^m/d)\, \psi S_t^{yf} \right) \right)$$

(where α is the bias-correction factor for reproductive rates). We estimated ω and α by determining the values of these parameters that minimized the sum of squared differences between observed and predicted population sizes. Based on this analysis, $\omega = 0.836$ and $\alpha = 0.701$, suggesting a positive bias in survival or reproductive rates. However, because of the limited number of years available for comparing observed and predicted population sizes, we also retained the balance equation that assumes estimates of survival and reproductive rates are unbiased.

Survival Process

For purposes of AHM, annual survival rates must be predicted based on the specification of regulation-specific harvest rates (and perhaps on other uncontrolled factors). Annual survival for each age (i) and sex (j) class under a given regulatory alternative is:

$$S_t^{i,j} = \bar{\theta}^j \left(1 - \frac{h_t^{am} \nu^{i,j}}{1-c} \right)$$

where:

S = annual survival,

$\bar{\theta}^j$ = mean survival from natural causes,

h^{am} = harvest rate of adult males,

ν = harvest vulnerability relative to adult males, and

c = rate of crippling (unretrieved harvest).

This model assumes that annual variation in survival is due solely to variation in harvest rates, that relative harvest vulnerability of the different age and sex classes is fixed and known, and that survival from natural causes is fixed at its sample mean. We estimated $\bar{\theta}^j = 0.7307$ and 0.5950 for males and females, respectively.

Reproductive process

As with survival, annual reproductive rates must be predicted in advance of setting regulations. We relied on the apparent relationship between breeding-population size and reproductive rates:

$$R_t = ae^{bN_t}$$

where R_t is the reproductive rate (i.e., A_t^m/d), N_t is breeding-population size in millions, and a and b are model parameters. The least-squares parameter estimates were $a = 2.508$ and $b = -0.875$. Because of both the importance and uncertainty of the relationship between population size and reproduction, we specified two alternative models in which the slope (b) was fixed at the least-squares estimate $\pm$ one standard error, and in which the intercepts (a) were subsequently re-estimated. This provided alternative hypotheses of strongly density-dependent ($a = 4.154$, $b = -1.377$) and weakly density-dependent reproduction ($a = 1.518$, $b = -0.373$).

Variance of Prediction Errors

Using the balance equations and sub-models provided above, predictions of breeding-population size in year $t+1$ depend only on the specification of a regulatory alternative and on an estimate of population size in year t. For the period in which comparisons were possible (1991–96), we were interested in how well these

38

predictions corresponded with observed population sizes. In making these comparisons, we were primarily concerned with how well the bias-corrected balance equations and reproductive and survival sub-models performed. Therefore, we relied on estimates of harvest rates rather than regulations as model inputs.

We estimated the prediction-error variance by setting:

$$e_t = \ln\left(N_t^{obs}\right) - \ln\left(N_t^{pre}\right)$$

$$\text{then assuming} \quad e_t \sim N\left(0, \sigma^2\right)$$

$$\text{and estimating} \quad \hat{\sigma}^2 = \sum_t \left[\ln\left(N_t^{obs}\right) - \ln\left(N_t^{pre}\right)\right]^2 / n$$

where N^{obs} and N^{pre} are observed and predicted population sizes (in millions), respectively, and $n = 6$. Variance estimates were similar regardless of whether we assumed that the bias was in reproductive rates or in survival, or whether we assumed that reproduction was strongly or weakly density-dependent. Thus, we averaged variance estimates to provide a final estimate of $\sigma^2 = 0.006$, which is equivalent to a coefficient of variation (CV) of 8.0%. We were concerned, however, about the small number of years available for estimating this variance. Therefore, we estimated an 80% confidence interval for σ^2 based on a Chi-squared distribution and used the upper limit for $\sigma^2 = 0.018$ (i.e., $CV = 14.5\%$) to express the additional uncertainty about the magnitude of prediction errors attributable to potentially important environmental effects not expressed by the models.

Model Implications

Model-specific regulatory strategies based on the hypothesis of weakly density-dependent reproduction are considerably more conservative than those based on the hypothesis of strongly density-dependent reproduction. The three models with weakly density-dependent reproduction suggest a carrying capacity (i.e., average population size in the absence of harvest) >2.0 million mallards, and prescribe extremely restrictive regulations for population size <1.0 million. The three models with strongly density-dependent reproduction suggest a carrying capacity of about 1.5 million mallards, and prescribe liberal regulations for population sizes >300 thousand. Optimal regulatory strategies are relatively insensitive to whether models include a bias correction or not. All model-specific regulatory strategies are "knife-edged", meaning that large differences in the optimal regulatory choice can be precipitated by only small changes in breeding-population size. This result is at least partially due to the small differences in predicted harvest rates among the current regulatory alternatives (see the section on Regulatory Alternatives).

Model Weights

We used Bayes' theorem to calculate model weights from a comparison of predicted and observed population sizes for the years 1997–2010. We calculated weights for the alternative models based on an assumption of equal model weights in 1996 (the last year data was used to develop most model components) and on estimates of year-specific harvest rates (Appendix E).

D WESTERN MALLARD MODELS

In contrast to mid-continent and eastern mallards, we did not model changes in population size for both the Alaska and California-Oregon stocks of western mallards as an explicit function of survival and reproductive rate estimates (which in turn may be functions of harvest and environmental covariates). We believed this so-called "balance-equation approach" was not viable for western mallards because of insufficient banding in Alaska to estimate survival rates, and because of the difficulty in estimating stock-specific fall age ratios from a sample of wings derived from a mix of breeding stocks.

Western Mallard Breeding Population Estimates

Table D.1 – Estimates (N) and associated standard errors (SE) of mallards (in millions) observed in Alaska (WBPHS strata 1–12) and California and Oregon (state surveys) combined.

Year	Alaska N	Alaska SE	California Oregon N	California Oregon SE	Total N	Total SE
1990	0.3669	0.0370				
1991	0.3853	0.0363				
1992	0.3457	0.0387	0.4835	0.0605	0.8292	0.0718
1993	0.2830	0.0295	0.4654	0.0510	0.7484	0.0589
1994	0.3509	0.0371	0.4367	0.0426	0.7876	0.0565
1995	0.5242	0.0680	0.4541	0.0428	0.9783	0.0803
1996	0.5220	0.0436	0.6451	0.0802	1.1671	0.0912
1997	0.5842	0.0520	0.6390	0.1043	1.2232	0.1166
1998	0.8362	0.0673	0.4868	0.0489	1.3230	0.0832
1999	0.7131	0.0696	0.6937	0.1066	1.4068	0.1273
2000	0.7703	0.0522	0.4639	0.0532	1.2342	0.0745
2001	0.7183	0.0541	0.4044	0.0451	1.1227	0.0705
2002	0.6673	0.0507	0.3775	0.0327	1.0449	0.0603
2003	0.8435	0.0668	0.4340	0.0501	1.2775	0.0835
2004	0.8111	0.0639	0.3547	0.0352	1.1658	0.0729
2005	0.7031	0.0547	0.4014	0.0474	1.1045	0.0724
2006	0.5158	0.0469	0.4879	0.0576	1.0037	0.0743
2007	0.5815	0.0551	0.4900	0.0546	1.0715	0.0775
2008	0.5324	0.0468	0.3814	0.0478	0.9138	0.0669
2009	0.5030	0.0449	0.3815	0.0639	0.8844	0.0781
2010	0.6056	0.0531	0.4430	0.0557	1.0485	0.0769

Model Structure

To evaluate western mallard population dynamics, we used a discrete logistic model (Schaefer 1954), which combines reproduction and natural mortality into a single parameter r, the intrinsic rate of growth. The model assumes density-dependent growth, which is regulated by the ratio of population size, N, to the carrying capacity of the environment, K (i.e., equilibrium population size in the absence of harvest). In the traditional formulation, harvest mortality is additive to other sources of mortality, but compensation for hunting losses can occur through subsequent increases in production. However, we parameterized the model in a way that also allows for compensation of harvest mortality between the hunting and breeding seasons. It is important to note that compensation modeled in this way is purely phenomenological, in the sense that there is no explicit ecological mechanism for compensation (e.g., density-dependent mortality after the hunting season). The basic model for both the Alaska and California-Oregon stocks has the form:

$$N_{t+1} = \left[N_t + N_t r \left(1 - \frac{N_t}{K} \right) \right] (1 - \alpha_t)$$

where,

$$\alpha_t = d h_t^{AM}$$

and where t = year, h^{AM} = the harvest rate of adult males, and d = a scaling factor. The scaling factor is used to account for a combination of unobservable effects, including un-retrieved harvest (i.e., crippling loss), differential harvest mortality of cohorts other than adult males, and for the possibility that some harvest mortality may not affect subsequent breeding-population size (i.e., the compensatory mortality hypothesis).

Estimation Framework

We used Bayesian estimation methods in combination with a state-space model that accounts explicitly for both process and observation error in breeding population size. This combination of methods is becoming widely used in natural resource modeling, in part because it facilitates the fitting of non-linear models that may have non-normal errors (Meyer and Millar 1999). The Bayesian approach also provides a natural and intuitive way to portray uncertainty, allows one to incorporate prior information about model parameters, and permits the updating of parameter estimates as further information becomes available.

We first scaled N by K as recommended by Meyer and Millar (1999), and assumed that process errors et were log-normally distributed with mean 0 and variance σ^2. Thus, the process model had the form:

$$P_t = N_t / K_t$$

$$\log(P_t) = \log \left([P_{t-1} + P_{t-1} r (1 - P_{t-1})] \left(1 - d h_{t-1}^{AM} \right) \right) + e_t$$

where,

$$e_t \sim N(0, \sigma^2)$$

The observation model related the unknown population sizes $(P_t K)$ to the population sizes (N_t) estimated from the breeding-population surveys in Alaska and California-Oregon. We assumed that the observation process yielded additive, normally distributed errors, which were represented by:

$$N_t = P_t K + \varepsilon_t^{BPOP},$$

where,

$$\varepsilon_t^{BPOP} \sim N(0, \sigma_{BPOP}^2).$$

permitting us to estimate the process error, which reflects the inability of the model to completely describe changes in population size. The process error reflects the combined effect of misspecification of an appropriate model form, as well as any un-modeled environmental drivers. We initially examined a number of possible environmental covariates, including the Palmer Drought Index in California and Oregon, spring temperature in Alaska, and the El Niño Southern Oscillation Index (http://www.cdc.noaa.gov/people/klaus.wolter/MEI/mei.html). While the estimated effects of these covariates on r or K were generally what one would expect, they were never of sufficient magnitude to have a meaningful effect on optimal harvest strategies. We therefore chose not to further pursue an investigation of environmental covariates, and posited that the process error was a sufficient surrogate for these un-modeled effects. Parameterization of the models also required measures of harvest rate. Beginning in 2002, harvest rates of adult males were estimated directly from the recovery of reward bands. Prior to 1993, we used direct recoveries of standard bands, corrected for band-reporting rates provided by Nichols et al. (1995b). We also used the band-reporting rates provided by Nichols et al. (1995b) for estimating harvest rates in 1994 and 1995, except that we inflated the reporting rates of full-address and toll-free bands based on an unpublished analysis by Clint Moore and Jim Nichols (Patuxent Wildlife Research Center). We were unwilling to estimate harvest rates for the years 1996–2001 because of suspected, but unknown, increases in the reporting rates of all bands. For simplicity, harvest rate estimates were treated as known values in our analysis, although future analyses might benefit from an appropriate observation model for these data.

In a Bayesian analysis, one is interested in making probabilistic statements about the model parameters (θ), conditioned on the observed data. Thus, we are interested in evaluating $P(\theta|data)$, which requires the specification of prior distributions for all model parameters and unobserved system states (θ) and the sampling distribution (likelihood) of the observed data $P(data|\theta)$. Using Bayes theorem, we can represent the posterior probability distribution of model parameters, conditioned on the data, as:

$$P(\theta|data) \propto P(\theta) \times P(data|\theta)$$

Accordingly, we specified prior distributions for model parameters r, K, d, and P_0, which is the initial population size relative to carrying capacity. For both stocks, we specified the following prior distributions for r, d, and σ^2:

$$
\begin{aligned}
r &\sim Lognormal(-1.0397, 1.4427) \\
d &\sim Uniform(0, 2) \\
\sigma^2 &\sim Inverse-gamma(0.001, 0.001)
\end{aligned}
$$

The prior distribution for r is centered at 0.35, which we believe to be a reasonable value for mallards based on life-history characteristics and estimates for other avian species. Yet the distribution also admits considerable uncertainty as to the value of r within what we believe to be realistic biological bounds. As for the harvest-rate scalar, we would expect $d \geq 1$ under the additive hypothesis and $d < 1$ under the compensatory hypothesis. As we had no data to specify an informative prior distribution, we specified a vague prior in which d could take on a wide range of values with equal probability. We used a traditional, uninformative prior distribution for σ^2. Prior distributions for K and P_0 were stock-specific and are described in the following sections.

We used the public-domain software WinBUGS (http://www.mrc-bsu.cam.ac.uk/bugs/) to derive samples from the joint posterior distribution of model parameters via Markov-Chain Monte Carlo (MCMC) simulations. We obtained 510,000 samples from the joint posterior distribution, discarded the first 10,000, and then thinned the remainder by 50, resulting in a final sample of 10,000.

Alaska mallards

Data selection—Breeding population estimates of mallards in Alaska (and the Old Crow Flats in Yukon) are available since 1955 in WBPHS strata 1–12 (Smith 1995). However, a change in survey aircraft in 1977 instantaneously increased the detectability of waterfowl, and thus population estimates (Hodges et al. 1996). Moreover, there was a rapid increase in average annual temperature in Alaska at the same time, apparently tied to changes in the frequency and intensity of El Niño events (http://www.cdc.noaa.gov/people/klaus.wolter/MEI/mei.html). This confounding of changes in climate and survey methods led us to truncate the years 1955–1977 from the time series of population estimates.

Modeling of the Alaska stock also depended on the availability of harvest-rate estimates derived from band-recovery data. Unfortunately, sufficient numbers of mallards were not banded in Alaska prior to 1990. A search for covariates that would have allowed us to make harvest-rate predictions for years in which band-recovery data were not available was not fruitful, and we were thus forced to further restrict the time series to 1990 and later. Even so, harvest rate estimates were not available for the years 1996–2001 because of unknown changes in band-reporting rates. Because available estimates of harvest rate showed no apparent variation over time, we simply used the mean and standard deviation of the available estimates and generated independent samples of predictions for the missing years based on a logit transformation and an assumption of normality:

$$ln\left(\frac{h_t}{1-h_t}\right) \sim Normal(-2.3434, 0.0778) \quad \text{for } t = 1996\text{--}2001$$

Prior distributions for K and P_0—We believed that sufficient information was available to use mildly informative priors for K and P_0. In recent years the Alaska stock has contained approximately 0.8 million mallards. If harvest rates have been comparable to that necessary to achieve maximum sustained yield (MSY) under the logistic model (i.e., $r/2$), then we would expect $K \approx 1.6$ million. On the other hand, if harvest rates have been less than those associated with MSY, then we would expect $K < 1.6$ million. Because we believed it was not likely that harvest rates were $> r/2$, we believed the likely range of K to be 0.8–1.6 million. We therefore specified a prior distribution that had a mean of 1.4 million, but had a sufficiently large variance to admit a wide range of possible values:

$$K \sim Lognormal(0.13035, 0.41224)$$

Extending this line of reasoning, we specified a prior distribution that assumed the estimated population size of approximately 0.4 million at the start of the time-series (i.e., 1990) was 20–60% of K. Thus on a log scale:

$$P_o \sim Uniform(-1.6094, -0.5108)$$

Parameter estimates—The logistic model and associated posterior parameter estimates provided a reasonable fit to the observed time-series of population estimates. The posterior means of K and r were similar to their priors, although their variances were considerably smaller (Table 1). However, the posterior distribution of d was essentially the same as its prior, reflecting the absence of information in the data necessary to reliably estimate this parameter.

Table D.2 – Estimates of model parameters resulting from fitting a discrete logistic model with MCMC to a time series of estimated population sizes and harvest rates of mallards breeding in Alaska, 1990–2009.

Parameter	Mean	SD	95% credibility interval
K	1.129	0.319	0.658–1.869
P_0	0.341	0.095	0.207–0.556
d	1.072	0.537	0.098–1.949
r	0.310	0.131	0.096–0.600
σ^2	0.023	0.013	0.007–0.056

California-Oregon mallards

Data selection—Breeding-population estimates of mallards in California are available starting in 1992, but not until 1994 in Oregon. Also, Oregon did not conduct a survey in 2001. To avoid truncating the time series, we used the admittedly weak relationship ($P = 0.07$) between California and Oregon population estimates to predict population sizes in Oregon in 1992, 1993, and 2001. The fitted linear model was:

$$N_t^{OR} = 68937 + 0.0961(N_t^{CA})$$

To derive realistic standard errors, we assumed that the predictions had the same mean coefficient of variation as the years when surveys were conducted ($n = 15$, $CV = 0.082$). The estimated sizes and variances of the CaliforniaOregon stock were calculated by simply summing the state-specific estimates.

We pooled banding and recovery data for California and Oregon and estimated harvest rates in the same manner as that for Alaska mallards. Although banded sample sizes were sufficient in all years, harvest rates could not be estimated for the years 1996–2001 because of unknown changes in band-reporting rates. As with Alaska, available estimates of harvest rate showed no apparent trend over time, and we simply used the mean and standard deviation of the available estimates and generated independent samples of predictions for the missing years based on a logit transformation and an assumption of normality:

$$ln\left(\frac{h_t}{1 - h_t}\right) \sim Normal(-2.2485, 0.1811) \quad \text{for } t = 1996\text{–}2001$$

Prior distributions for K and P_0—Unlike the Alaska stock, the California-Oregon population has been relatively stable with a mean of 0.48 million mallards. We believed K should be in the range 0.48–0.96 million, assuming the logistic model and that harvest rates were $\leq r/2$. We therefore specified a prior distribution on K that had a mean of 0.7 million, but with a variance sufficiently large to admit a wide range of possible values:

$$K \sim Lognormal(-0.5628, 0.41224)$$

The estimated size of the California-Oregon stock was 0.48 million at the start of the time-series (i.e., 1992). We used a similar line of reasoning as that for Alaska for specifying a prior distribution P_0, positing that initial population size was 40-100% of K. Thus on a log scale:

$$P_o \sim Uniform(-0.9163, 0.0)$$

44

Table D.3 – Estimates of model parameters resulting from fitting a discrete logistic model with MCMC to a time-series of estimated population sizes and harvest rates of mallards breeding in California and Oregon, 1992–2009.

Parameter	Mean	SD	95% credibility interval
K	0.636	0.172	0.440–1.095
P_0	0.757	0.158	0.436–0.988
d	0.585	0.404	0.033–1.577
r	0.331	0.227	0.064–0.916
σ^2	0.013	0.012	0.001–0.043

Parameter estimates—The logistic model and associated posterior parameter estimates provided a reasonable fit to the observed time series of population estimates. The posterior means of K and r were similar to their priors, although the variances were considerably smaller (Table 2). Interestingly, the posterior mean of d was < 1, suggestive of a compensatory response to harvest; however the standard deviation of the estimate was large, with the upper 95% credibility limit > 1.

For each western mallard substock, we further summarized the simulation results for r, K, and the scaling factor d to admit parametric uncertainty with a formal correlation structure within the optimization procedure used to calculate the harvest strategy. We first defined a joint distribution for 3 discrete outcomes for each of the 3 population parameters. We used the 30 and 70 percent quantiles for each parameter as the cut points to define three bins for which to discretize 3 values of each posterior distribution. We then determined the frequency of occurrence of each of the 27 possible combinations of each parameter value falling within the 3 bins from the MCMC simulation results. These frequencies were then assigned parameter values based on the midpoint of bin ranges (15, 50, 85 percent quantiles) to specify the joint distribution of the population parameter values used in the optimization.

E MODELING MALLARD HARVEST RATES

Mid-continent

We modeled harvest rates of mid-continent mallards within a Bayesian hierarchical framework. We developed a set of models to predict harvest rates under each regulatory alternative as a function of the harvest rates observed under the liberal alternative, using historical information. We modeled the probability of regulation-specific harvest rates (h) based on normal distributions with the following parameterizations:

$$\text{Closed:} \quad p(h_C) \sim N(\mu_C, \nu_C^2)$$

$$\text{Restrictive:} \quad p(h_R) \sim N(\mu_R, \nu_R^2)$$

$$\text{Moderate:} \quad p(h_M) \sim N(\mu_M, \nu_M^2)$$

$$\text{Liberal:} \quad p(h_L) \sim N(\mu_L, \nu_L^2)$$

For the restrictive and moderate alternatives we introduced the parameter γ to represent the relative difference between the harvest rate observed under the liberal alternative and the moderate or restrictive alternatives. Based on this parameterization, we are making use of the information that has been gained (under the liberal alternative) and are modeling harvest rates for the restrictive and moderate alternatives as a function of the mean harvest rate observed under the liberal alternative. For the harvest-rate distributions assumed under the restrictive and moderate regulatory alternatives, we specified that γ_R and γ_M are equal to the prior estimates of the predicted mean harvest rates under the restrictive and moderate alternatives divided by the prior estimates of the predicted mean harvest rates observed under the liberal alternative. Thus, these parameters act to scale the mean of the restrictive and moderate distributions in relation to the mean harvest rate observed under the liberal regulatory alternative. We also considered the marginal effect of framework-date extensions under the moderate and liberal alternatives by including the parameter δ_f.

To update the probability distributions of harvest rates realized under each regulatory alternative, we first needed to specify a prior probability distribution for each of the model parameters. These distributions represent prior beliefs regarding the relationship between each regulatory alternative and the expected harvest rates. We used a normal distribution to represent the mean and a scaled inverse-chi-square distribution to represent the variance of the normal distribution of the likelihood. For the mean (μ) of each harvest-rate distribution associated with each regulatory alternative, we use the predicted mean harvest rates provided in (U. S. Fish and Wildlife Service 2000, 13–14), assuming uniformity of regulatory prescriptions across flyways. We set prior values of each standard deviation (ν) equal to 20% of the mean ($CV = 0.2$) based on an analysis by Johnson et al. (1997). We then specified the following prior distributions and parameter values under each regulatory package:

Closed (in U.S. only):

$$p(\mu_C) \sim N\left(0.0088, \frac{0.0018^2}{6}\right)$$

$$p(\nu_C^2) \sim Scaled\ Inv - \chi^2(6, 0.0018^2)$$

These closed-season parameter values are based on observed harvest rates in Canada during the 1988–93 seasons, which was a period of restrictive regulations in both Canada and the United States.

For the restrictive and moderate alternatives, we specified that the standard error of the normal distribution of the scaling parameter is based on a coefficient of variation for the mean equal to 0.3. The scale parameter of the inverse-chi-square distribution was set equal to the standard deviation of the harvest rate mean under the restrictive and moderate regulation alternatives (i.e., $CV = 0.2$).

Restrictive:

$$p(\gamma_R) \sim N\left(0.51, \frac{0.15^2}{6}\right)$$

$$p(\nu_R^2) \sim Scaled\,Inv - \chi^2(6, 0.0133^2)$$

Moderate:

$$p(\gamma_M) \sim N\left(0.85, \frac{0.26^2}{6}\right)$$

$$p(\nu_r^2) \sim Scaled\,Inv - \chi^2(6, 0.0222^2)$$

Liberal:

$$p(\mu_L) \sim N\left(0.1305, \frac{0.0261^2}{6}\right)$$

$$p(\nu_R^2) \sim Scaled\,Inv - \chi^2(6, 0.0261^2)$$

The prior distribution for the marginal effect of the framework-date extension was specified as:

$$p(\delta_f) \sim N\left(0.02, 0.01^2\right)$$

The prior distributions were multiplied by the likelihood functions based on the last 12 years of data under liberal regulations, and the resulting posterior distributions were evaluated with Markov Chain Monte Carlo simulation. Posterior estimates of model parameters and of annual harvest rates are provided in Table E.1.

Table E.1 – Parameter estimates for predicting mid-continent mallard harvest rates resulting from a hierarchical, Bayesian analysis of mid-continent mallard banding and recovery information from 1998–2009.

Parameter	Estimate	SD	Parameter	Estimate	SD
μ_C	0.0088	0.0021	h_{1998}	0.1019	0.0070
ν_C	0.0019	0.0005	h_{1999}	0.0980	0.0071
γ_R	0.5105	0.0607	h_{2000}	0.1247	0.0084
ν_R	0.0129	0.0032	h_{2001}	0.0920	0.0088
γ_M	0.8501	0.1086	h_{2002}	0.1124	0.0060
ν_M	0.0216	0.0055	h_{2003}	0.1128	0.0069
μ_L	0.1095	0.0067	h_{2004}	0.1193	0.0109
ν_L	0.0197	0.0035	h_{2005}	0.1151	0.0085
δ_f	0.0070	0.0074	h_{2006}	0.1091	0.0078
			h_{2007}	0.1033	0.0065
			h_{2008}	0.1140	0.0068
			h_{2009}	0.0952	0.0081

Eastern

We modeled harvest rates of eastern mallards using the same parameterizations as those for mid-continent mallards:

$$
\begin{aligned}
\text{Closed:} \quad & p(h_C) \sim N(\mu_C, \nu_C^2) \\
\text{Restrictive:} \quad & p(h_R) \sim N(\gamma_R \mu_L, \nu_R^2) \\
\text{Moderate:} \quad & p(h_M) \sim N(\gamma_M \mu_L + \delta_f, \nu_M^2) \\
\text{Liberal:} \quad & p(h_L) \sim N(\mu_L + \delta_f, \nu_L^2)
\end{aligned}
$$

We set prior values of each standard deviation (ν) equal to 30% of the mean ($CV = 0.3$) to account for additional variation due to changes in regulations in the other Flyways and their unpredictable effects on the harvest rates of eastern mallards. We then specified the following prior distribution and parameter values for the liberal regulatory alternative:

Closed (in US only):

$$p(\mu_C) \sim N\left(0.08, \frac{0.024^2}{6}\right)$$

$$p(\nu_C^2) \sim Scaled\,Inv - \chi^2(6, 0.024^2)$$

Restrictive:

$$p(\gamma_R) \sim N\left(0.076, \frac{0.228^2}{6}\right)$$

$$p(\nu_R^2) \sim Scaled\,Inv - \chi^2(6, 0.0404^2)$$

Moderate:

$$p(\gamma_M) \sim N\left(0.92, \frac{0.28^2}{6}\right)$$

$$p(\nu_R^2) \sim Scaled\,Inv - \chi^2(6, 0.0488^2)$$

Liberal:

$$p(\mu_L) \sim N\left(0.1771, \frac{0.0531^2}{6}\right)$$

$$p(\nu_R^2) \sim Scaled\,Inv - \chi^2(6, 0.0531^2)$$

A previous analysis suggested that the effect of the framework-date extension on eastern mallards would be of lower magnitude and more variable than on mid-continent mallards (U. S. Fish and Wildlife Service 2000). Therefore, we specified the following prior distribution for the marginal effect of the framework-date extension for eastern mallards as:

$$p(\delta_f) \sim N\left(0.01, 0.01^2\right)$$

The prior distributions were multiplied by the likelihood functions based on the last 8 years of data under liberal regulations, and the resulting posterior distributions were evaluated with Markov Chain Monte Carlo simulation. Posterior estimates of model parameters and of annual harvest rates are provided in Table E.2.

Table E.2 – Parameter estimates for predicting eastern mallard harvest rates resulting from a hierarchical, Bayesian analysis of eastern mallard banding and recovery information from 2002–2009.

Parameter	Estimate	SD	Parameter	Estimate	SD
μ_C	0.0801	0.0254	h_{2002}	0.1613	0.0125
ν_C	0.0232	0.0058	h_{2003}	0.1458	0.0105
γ_R	0.7606	0.0910	h_{2004}	0.1359	0.0114
ν_R	0.0392	0.0099	h_{2005}	0.1308	0.0120
γ_M	0.9204	0.1149	h_{2006}	0.1036	0.0132
ν_M	0.0475	0.0137	h_{2007}	0.1223	0.0133
μ_L	0.1445	0.0144	h_{2008}	0.1206	0.0119
ν_L	0.0418	0.0080	h_{2009}	0.1384	0.0134
δ_f	0.0031	0.0094			

Western

We modeled harvest rates of western mallards using a similar parameterization as that used for mid-continent and eastern mallards. However, we did not explicitly model the effect of the framework date extension because we did not use data observed prior to when framework date extensions were available. In the western mallard parameterization, the effect of the framework date extensions are implicit in the expected mean harvest rate expected under the liberal regulatory option.

$$
\begin{aligned}
\text{Closed:} \quad & p(h_C) \sim N(\mu_C, \nu_C^2) \\
\text{Restrictive:} \quad & p(h_R) \sim N(\gamma_R \mu_L, \nu_R^2) \\
\text{Moderate:} \quad & p(h_M) \sim N(\gamma_M \mu_L, \nu_M^2) \\
\text{Liberal:} \quad & p(h_L) \sim N(\mu_L, \nu_L^2)
\end{aligned}
$$

We set prior values of each standard deviation (ν) equal to 30% of the mean ($CV=0.3$) to account for additional variation due to changes in regulations in the other Flyways and their unpredictable effects on the harvest rates of western mallards. We then specified the following prior distribution and parameter values for the liberal regulatory alternative:

Closed (in US only):

$$p(\mu_C) \sim N\left(0.01, \frac{0.00264^2}{6}\right)$$

$$p(\nu_C^2) \sim Scaled\,Inv - \chi^2(6, 0.00264^2)$$

Restrictive:

$$p(\gamma_R) \sim N\left(0.51, \frac{0.153^2}{6}\right)$$

$$p(\nu_R^2) \sim Scaled\,Inv - \chi^2(6, 0.01683^2)$$

Moderate:

$$p(\gamma_M) \sim N\left(0.85, \frac{0.255^2}{6}\right)$$

$$p(\nu_R^2) \sim Scaled\,Inv - \chi^2(6, 0, 0.02805^2)$$

Liberal:

$$p(\mu_L) \sim N\left(0.11, \frac{0.033^2}{6}\right)$$

$$p(\nu_R^2) \sim Scaled\,Inv - \chi^2(6, 0.033^2)$$

The prior distributions were multiplied by the likelihood functions based on the last 2 years of data under liberal regulations, and the resulting posterior distributions were evaluated with Markov Chain Monte Carlo simulation. Posterior estimates of model parameters and of annual harvest rates are provided Table E.3.

Table E.3 – Parameter estimates for predicting western mallard harvest rates resulting from a hierarchical, Bayesian analysis of western mallard banding and recovery information from 2008–2009.

Parameter	Estimate	SD	Parameter	Estimate	SD
μ_C	0.0097	0.0189	h_{2008}	0.1350	0.0199
ν_C	0.0182	0.0046	h_{2009}	0.1182	0.0161
γ_R	0.5116	0.0612			
ν_R	0.0163	0.0041			
γ_M	0.8505	0.1023			
ν_M	0.0271	0.0069			
μ_L	0.1149	0.0120			
ν_L	0.0306	0.0071			

F   NORTHERN PINTAIL MODELS

The Flyway Councils have long identified the northern pintail as a high-priority species for inclusion in the AHM process. In 2010, the USFWS and Flyway Councils adopted an adaptive management framework to inform northern pintail harvest management. A detailed progress report that describes the evolution of the pintail harvest strategy is available online (http://www.fws.gov/migratorybirds/NewsPublicationsReports.html). The northern pintail adaptive harvest management protocol considers two population models that represent alternative hypotheses about the effect of harvest on population dynamics: one in which harvest is additive to natural mortality, and another in which harvest is compensatory to natural mortality. We describe the technical details of the northern pintail model set below.

Latitude Bias Correction Model

Northern pintails tend to settle on breeding territories farther north during years when the prairies are dry and farther south during wet years. When pintails settle farther north, a smaller proportion are counted during the Waterfowl Breeding Population and Habitat Survey (WBPHS strata: 1–50, 75–77), thus the population estimate is biased low in comparison to years when the birds settle farther south. This phenomenon may be a result of decreased detectability of pintails during surveys in northern latitudes compared to southern latitudes or because birds settle in regions not covered by the survey. Runge and Boomer (2005) developed an empirical relationship to correct the observed breeding population estimates for this bias. Based on this approach, the latitude-adjusted breeding population size ($cBPOP_{t+1}$) in year t, can be calculated with

$$cBPOP_t = e^{ln(oBPOP_t) + 0.741(mLAT_t - 51.68)}$$

where $oBPOP_t$ is the observed breeding population size in year t and $mLAT_t$ is the mean latitude of the observed breeding population in year t. The mean latitude of the pintail breeding population distribution is based on the geographical centroid of each stratum in the traditional survey area (WBPHS strata: 1–50, 75–77). In year t, we calculate a mean latitude ($mLAT_t$) weighted by the population estimates from each strata with

$$mLAT_t = \sum_j [Lat_j(oBPOP_{t,j}/oBPOP_t)]$$

where Lat_j is the latitude of survey stratum j.

Population Models

Two population models are considered: one in which harvest is additive to natural mortality, and another in which harvest is compensatory to natural mortality. The models differ in how they handle the winter survival rate. In the additive model, winter survival rate is a constant, whereas winter survival is density-dependent in the compensatory model.

For the additive harvest mortality model, the latitude-adjusted population size ($cBPOP$) in year $t + 1$, is calculated with

$$cBPOP_{t+1} = \left(cBPOP_t s_s \left(1 + \gamma_R \hat{R}_t \right) - \frac{\hat{H}_t}{(1 - c)} \right) s_w$$

51

where $cBPOP_t$ is the latitude-adjusted breeding population size in year t, s_s and s_w are the summer and winter survival rates, respectively, γ_R is a bias-correction constant for the age-ratio, c is the crippling loss rate, $\hat{R}_t$ is the predicted age-ratio, and $\hat{H}_t$ is the predicted continental harvest. The model uses the following constants: $s_s = 0.70$, $s_w = 0.93$, $\gamma_R = 0.8$, and $c = 0.20$.

The compensatory harvest mortality model serves as a hypothesis that stands in contrast to the additive harvest mortality model, positing a strong but realistic degree of compensation. The compensatory model assumes that the mechanism for compensation is density-dependent post-harvest (winter) survival (Runge 2007). The form is a logistic relationship between winter survival and post-harvest population size, with the relationship anchored around the historic mean values for each variable. For the compensatory model, predicted winter survival rate in year t (s_t) is calculated as

$$s_t = s_0 + (s_1 - s_0)\left[1 + e^{-(a + b(P_t - \bar{P}))}\right]^{-1},$$

where s_1 (upper asymptote) is 1.0, s_0 (lower asymptote) is 0.7, b (slope term) is -1.0, P_t is the post-harvest population size in year t (expressed in millions), $\bar{P}$ is the mean post-harvest population size (4.295 million from 1974 through 2005), and

$$a = \text{logit}\left(\frac{\bar{s} - s_0}{s_1 - s_0}\right)$$

or

$$a = \log\left(\frac{\bar{s} - s_0}{s_1 - s_0}\right) - \log\left\{1 - \left(\frac{\bar{s} - s_0}{s_1 - s_0}\right)\right\},$$

where $\bar{s}$ is 0.93 (mean winter survival rate).

Age Ratio Submodel

Recruitment ($\hat{R}$) in year t is measured by the vulnerability-adjusted, female age-ratio in the fall population and is predicted as

$$\hat{R}_t = e^{(7.6048 - 0.13183 mLAT_t - 0.09212 cBPOP_t)}$$

where $mLAT_t$ is the mean latitude of the observed breeding population in year t and $cBPOP_t$ is the latitude-adjusted breeding population in year t (expressed in millions).

Harvest Submodel

Predicted continental harvest ($\hat{H}$) in year t is calculated with

$$\hat{H}_t = H_{PF} + H_{CF} + H_{MF} + H_{AF} + H_{AKCan}$$

where H_{PF}, H_{CF}, H_{MF}, and H_{AF} are the predicted harvest in the Pacific, Central, Mississippi, and Atlantic Flyways, respectively. The expected harvest from Alaska and Canada H_{AKCan} is assumed fixed and equal to 67,000 birds. Flyway specific harvest predictions are calculated with

$$H_{PF} = -12051.41 + 1160.960 days + 73911.49 bag$$

$$H_{CF} = -95245.20 + 2946.285 days + 15228.03 bag + 23136.04 sis$$

$$H_{MF} = -59083.66 + 3413.49 days + 7911.95 bag + 59510.10 sis$$

$$H_{PF} = -2403.06 + 360.950 days + 5494.00 bag$$

where *days* is the season length, *bag* is the daily bag limit, and *sis* is an indicator variable with value equal to 0 (full season equal to length from general duck season) or 1 (restrictive season within the liberal or moderate regulatory alternative for general duck season, i.e., partial season).

Model Weights

The relative degree of confidence that we have in the additive or compensatory mortality hypothesis can be represented with model weights that are updated annually from a comparison of model specific predictions and observed population sizes. For the period 1974–2009, the subsequent year's breeding population size (on the latitude-adjusted scale) was predicted with both the additive and compensatory models, and compared to the observed breeding population size (on the latitude-adjusted scale). The mean-squared error of the predictions from the additive model (MSE_{add}) was calculated as:

$$MSE_{add} = \frac{1}{(t - 1975) + 1} \sum_{t=1975}^{t} \left(cBPOP_t - cBPOP_t^{add} \right)^2,$$

and the mean-squared error of the predictions from the compensatory model were calculated in a similar manner.

We calculated model weights for the additive and compensatory model as a function of their relative mean-squared errors. The model weight for the additive model (W_{add}) was determined by

$$W_{add} = \frac{\dfrac{1}{MSE_{add}}}{\dfrac{1}{MSE_{add}} + \dfrac{1}{MSE_{comp}}}$$

The model weight for the compensatory model was found in a corresponding manner, or by subtracting the additive model weight from 1.0. As of 2010, the compensatory model did not fit the historic data as well as the additive model; the model weights were 0.596 for the additive model and 0.404 for the compensatory model, unchanged from 2007.

Equilibrium Conditions

Equilibrium analyses of the additive model suggest a carrying capacity of 7.32 million (on the latitude-adjusted scale), maximum sustained yield (MSY) of 444,000 at an equilibrium population size of 3.34 million, and harvest rate of 10.7% (Runge and Boomer 2005). The yield curve resulting from the compensatory model is significantly skewed compared to the additive model (Figure F.1). Compared to the additive model, the compensatory model results in a lower carrying capacity (4.67 million), a higher MSY (560 thousand) at a lower equilibrium population size (3.00 million), and a higher maximum harvest rate (14.8%).

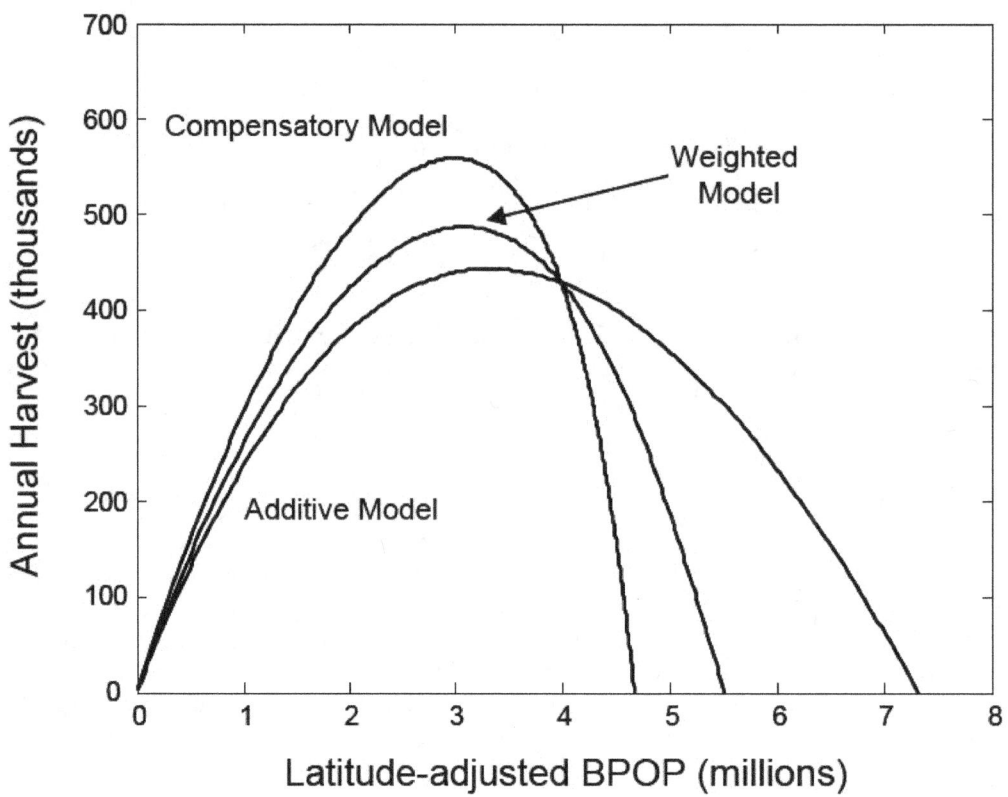

Figure F.1 – Harvest yield curves resulting from an equilibrium analysis of the northern pintail model set based on 2010 model weights.

The average model, based on 2010 model weights, produces a yield curve that is intermediate between the additive and compensatory models. An equilibrium analysis of the weighted model results in carrying capacity, MSY, equilibrium population size at MSY, and maximum harvest rate that are intermediate between the additive and compensatory model results (5.50 million, 488 thousand, 3.08 million, and 12.6% respectively).

G SCAUP MODEL

We use a state-space formulation of scaup population and harvest dynamics within a Bayesian estimation framework (Meyer and Millar 1999, Millar and Meyer 2000). This analytical framework allows us to represent uncertainty associated with the monitoring programs (observation error) and the ability of our model formulation to predict actual changes in the system (process error).

Process Model

Given a logistic growth population model that includes harvest (Schaefer 1954), scaup population and harvest dynamics are calculated as a function of the intrinsic rate of increase (r), carrying capacity (K), and harvest (H_t). Following Meyer and Millar (1999), we scaled population sizes by K (i.e., $P_t = N_t/K$) and assumed that process errors (ϵ_t) are lognormally distributed with a mean of 0 and variance $\sigma^2_{process}$. The state dynamics can be expressed as

$$P_{1974} = P_0 e^{\varepsilon_{1974}}$$

$$P_t = \left(P_{t-1} + rP_{t-1}\left(1 - P_{t-1}\right) - H_{t-1}/K\right)e^{\varepsilon_t}, \quad t = 1975, \ldots, 2009,$$

where P_0 is the initial ratio of population size to carrying capacity. To predict total scaup harvest levels, we modeled scaup harvest rates (h_t) as a function of the pooled direct recovery rate (f_t) observed each year with

$$h_t = f_t/\lambda_t.$$

We specified reporting rate (λ_t) distributions based on estimates for mallards (*Anas platyrhynchos*) from large scale historical and existing reward banding studies (Henny and Burnham 1976, Nichols et al. 1995*b*, P. Garrettson unpublished data). We accounted for increases in reporting rate believed to be associated with changes in band type (e.g., from AVISE and new address bands to 1-800 toll free bands) by specifying year specific reporting rates according to

$$\lambda_t \sim Normal(0.38, 0.04), \quad t = 1974, \ldots, 1996$$
$$\lambda_t \sim Normal(0.70, 0.04), \quad t = 1997, \ldots, 2009.$$

We then predicted total scaup harvest (H_t) with

$$H_t = h_t\left[P_t + rP + t\left(1 - P\right)\right]K, \quad t = 1974, \ldots, 2009.$$

Observation Model

We compared our predictions of population and harvest numbers from our process model to the observations collected by the Waterfowl and Breeding Habitat Survey (WBPHS) and the Harvest Survey programs with the following relationships, assuming that the population and harvest observation errors were additive and normally distributed. May breeding population estimates were related to model predictions by

$$N_t^{Observed} - P_t K = \varepsilon_t^{BPOP},$$

where

$$\varepsilon_t^{BPOP} \sim N(0, \sigma_{t,BPOP}^2), \quad t = 1974, \ldots, 2009,$$

where $\sigma_{t,BPOP}^2$ is specified each year with the BPOP variance estimates from the WBPHS.

We adjusted our harvest predictions to the observed harvest data estimates with a scaling parameter (q) according to

$$H_t^{Observed} - (h_t [P_t + rP_t (1-P)] K) / q = \varepsilon_t^H, \quad t = 1974, \ldots, 2009,$$

where,

$$\varepsilon_t^H \sim N(0, \sigma_{t,Harvest}^2).$$

We assumed that appropriate measures of the harvest observation error $\sigma_{t,Harvest}^2$ could be approximated by assuming a coefficient of variation for each annual harvest estimate equal to 0.15 (Paul Padding pers. comm.). The final component of the likelihood included the year specific direct recovery rates that were represented by the rate parameter (f_t) of a Binomial distribution indexed by the total number of birds banded preseason and estimated with,

$$f_t = m_t / M_t,$$

$$m_t \sim Binomial(M_t, f_t)$$

where m_t is the total number of scaup banded preseason in year t and recovered during the hunting season in year t and M_t is the total number of scaup banded preseason in year t.

Bayesian Analysis

Following Meyer and Millar (1999), we developed a fully conditional joint probability model, by first proposing prior distributions for all model parameters and unobserved system states and secondly by developing a fully conditional likelihood for each sampling distribution.

Prior Distributions

For this analysis, a joint prior distribution is required because the unknown system states P are assumed to be conditionally independent (Meyer and Millar 1999). This leads to the following joint prior distribution for the model parameters and unobserved system states

$$P(r, K, q, f_t, \lambda_t, \sigma_{Process}^2, P_0, P_{1,\ldots,T}) =$$
$$p(r)p(K)p(q)p(f_t)p(\lambda_t)p(\sigma_{Process}^2)p(P_0)p(P_1|P_0, \sigma_{Process}^2)$$
$$\times \prod_{t=2}^{n} p(P_t|P_{t-1}, r, K, f_{t-1}, \lambda_{t-1}, \sigma_{Process}^2)$$

In general, we chose non-informative priors to represent the uncertainty we have in specifying the value of the parameters used in our assessment. However, we were required to use existing information to specify informative priors for the initial ratio of population size to carrying capacity (P_0) as well as the reporting rate values (λ_t) specified above that were used to adjust the direct recovery rate estimates to harvest rates.

We specified that the value of P_0, ranged from the population size at maximum sustained yield ($P_0 = N_{MSY}/K = (K/2)/K = 0.5$) to the carrying capacity ($P_0 = N/K = 1$), using a uniform distribution on the log scale to represent this range of values. We assumed that the exploitation experienced at this population state was somewhere on the right-hand shoulder of a sustained yield curve (i.e., between MSY and K). Given that we have very little evidence to suggest that historical scaup harvest levels were limiting scaup population growth, this seems like a reasonable prior distribution.

We used non-informative prior distributions to represent the variance and scaling terms, while the priors for the population parameters r and K were chosen to be vague but within biological bounds. These distributions were specified according to

$$
\begin{aligned}
P_0 &\sim Uniform(ln(0.5), 0), \\
K &\sim Lognormal(2.17, 0.667), \\
r &\sim Uniform(0.00001, 2), \\
f_t &\sim Beta(0.5, 0.5), \\
q &\sim Uniform(0.0, 2), \\
\sigma^2_{Process} &\sim Inverse\ Gamma(0.001, 0.001).
\end{aligned}
$$

Likelihood

We related the observed population, total harvest estimates, and observed direct recoveries to the model parameters and unobserved system states with the following likelihood function:

$$
\begin{aligned}
P(N_{1,...,T}, H_{1,...,T}, m_{1,...,T} M_{1,...,T} | r, K, f_t, \lambda_t, q, \sigma^2_{Process}, \sigma^2_{Harvest}, P_{1,...,T}) = \\
\times \prod_{t=1}^{T} p(N_t | P_t, K, \sigma^2_{BPOP}) \times \prod_{t=1}^{T} p(H_t | P_t, r, K, q, f_t, \lambda_t, \sigma^2_{Harvest}) \\
\times \prod_{t=1}^{T} p(m_t | M_t, f_t)
\end{aligned}
$$

Posterior Evaluation

Using Bayes theorem we then specified a posterior distribution for the fully conditional joint probability distribution of the parameters given the observed information according to

$$
\begin{aligned}
P(r, K, q, f_t, \lambda_t, \sigma^2_{Process}, &P_0, P_{1,\ldots,T} | N_{1,\ldots,T}, H_{1,\ldots,T}, m_{1,\ldots,T}, M_{1,\ldots,T}) \propto \\
&p(r)p(K)p(q)p(f_t)p(\lambda_t)p(\sigma^2_{Process})p(P_0)p(P_1|P_0, \sigma^2_{Process}) \\
&\times \prod_{t=2}^{n} p(p|P_{t-1}, r, K, f_{t-1}, \lambda_{t-1}, \sigma^2_{Process}) \times \prod_{t=1}^{T} p(N_t|P_t, K, \sigma^2_{BPOP}) \\
&\times \prod_{t=1}^{T} p(H_t|P_t, r, K, q, f_t, \lambda_t, \sigma^2_{Harvest}) \times \prod_{t=1}^{T} p(m_t|M_t, f_t)
\end{aligned}
$$

We used Markov Chain Monte Carlo (MCMC) methods to evaluate the posterior distribution using WinBUGS (Spiegelhalter et al. 2003). We randomly generated initial values and simulated 5 independent chains each with 1,000,000 iterations. We discarded the first half of the simulation and thinned each chain by 250, yielding a sample of 10,000 points. We calculated Gelman-Rubin statistics (Brooks and Gelman 1998) to monitor for lack of convergence. The state space formulation and Bayesian analysis framework provided reasonable fits to the observed breeding population and total harvest estimates with realistic measures of variation. The 2010 posterior estimates of model parameters based on data from 1974–2009 are provided in Table G.1.

Table G.1 – Model parameter estimates resulting from a Bayesian analysis of scaup breeding population, harvest, and banding information from 1974–2009.

Parameter	Mean	2.5% CI	Median	97.5% CI
r	0.1222	0.0396	0.1127	0.2560
K	8.1716	5.7840	7.8115	12.1100
σ^2	0.0076	0.0025	0.0069	0.0165
q	0.5561	0.4838	0.5548	0.6344

We further summarized the simulation results for r, K, and the scaling parameter q to admit parametric uncertainty with a formal correlation structure within the optimization procedure used to calculate the harvest strategy. We first defined a joint distribution for 3 discrete outcomes for each of the 3 population parameters. We used the 30 and 70 percent quantiles for each parameter as the cut points to define three bins for which to discretize 3 values of each posterior distribution. We then determined the frequency of occurrence of each of the 27 possible combinations of each parameter value falling within the 3 bins from the MCMC simulation results. These frequencies were then assigned parameter values based on the midpoint of the bin ranges (15, 50, 85 percent quantiles) to specify the joint distribution of the population parameter values used in the optimization.

Division of Migratory Bird Management
11510 American Holly Dr.
Laurel, MD 20708-4016

U.S. Fish and Wildlife Service
http://www.fws.gov

For state transfer relay service
TTY/Voice: 711